DISCOVERY

CASTLES

Barbara Taylor

Consultant: William Klemperer

LORENZ BOOKS

First published in 2000 by Lorenz Books
© Anness Publishing Limited 2000
Lorenz Books is an imprint of Anness Publishing
Limited, Hermes House, 88-89 Blackfriars Road,
London SE1 8HA

This edition distributed in Canada by Raincoast Books,
8680 Cambie Street, Vancouver, British Columbia
V6P 6M9

ISBN 0 7548 0207 8

A CIP catalogue record for this book is available from
the British Library

Publisher: Joanna Lorenz
Managing Editor, Children's Books:
    Gilly Cameron Cooper
Assistant Editor: Jenni Rainford
Editorial Reader: Penelope Goodare
Series Design: John Jamieson
Designer: Ann Samuel
Illustration: Donato Spedaliere; Rob Chapman
and Clive Spong at Linden Artists
Picture Research: Kay Rowley
Photography: John Freeman
Stylists: Konika Shankar, Melanie Williams

Anness Publishing would like to thank the following
children, and their parents, for modelling for this book:
Hazel Askew, Danny Bill, Eleanor Grimshaw, Gigi
Playfair, Gemma Nelson, Isobel Nelson, Victoria
Sinton, Kwan Tualki

PICTURE CREDITS
AAA: fc, 4bl, 8br, 10br, 12bl, 14br, 17bl, 24bl, 24tl,
30bl, 34br, 39bl, 41br, 45bl, 44bl, 59cr; AKG: 5bl, 4tr,
11br, 25tl, 26bl, 27tr, 29cr, 45tr, 51bl, 51cr, 52bl, 60c,
20tl, 21bl; Bridgeman Art Library: 5tr, 11tr, 22bc, 25b,
28cr, 28bl, 34tr, 39tr, 40tr, 42bl, 45tl, 22bc, 21cl, 21br;
J. Allen Cash: 8bl, 8tr, 61br, 9br; Collections JSH: 57tr;
English Heritage: 11tl, 34br, 54bl, 14tc; ET Archive:
24br, 43tr, 17tl, tr; Fine Art: 5tl, 58bl; Ann Ronan at
Image Select: 3br, 9tr, 37tr, 50bl; Japan Archive: 39tl,
60tl; Mary Evans Picture Library: 10bl, 28tl, 29br, 29cr,
bc, 35tr, 38bl, 61, 38tr, 60tr, 40br, 41cl, cr, 44tl,
44br, 46bc, 49tc, cl, br, 51tl, 54tr, 21tr, 18bc, 16tl, br;
Michael Holford:2bl, 9tr, 48tl, bc, 59br, 15cl; National
Trust: 35tl, 49br, 54br, 15tr, br, 14tr; Royal Armouries:
fc, 45br, 49tl, 59bl, 59tr; Skyscan: 55c; Tony Stone
Images: 9bl; Trip Photography: 36bl, 55tl, 14bl;
Warwick Castle: 59tl; Werner Forman Archive:17cr.

Printed and bound in Singapore

10 9 8 7 6 5 4 3 2 1

CONTENTS

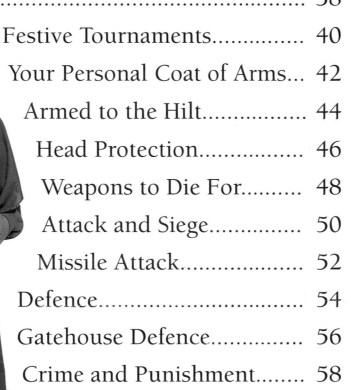

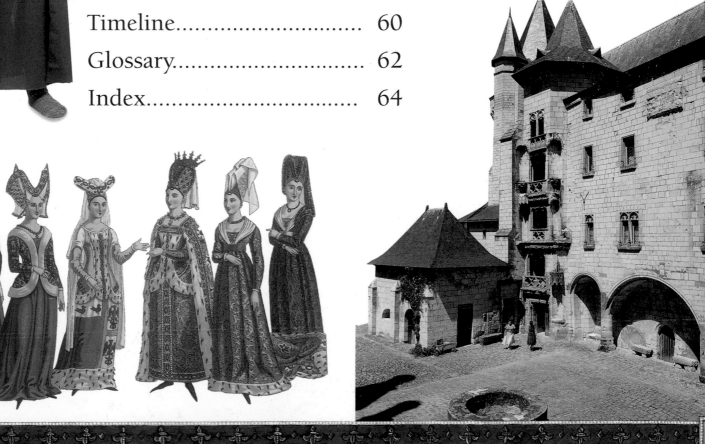

A Fortified Home

When most castles were built, 500 or more years ago, their mighty walls and towers dominated the countryside. It was clear to everyone who lived nearby that the owners were rich and powerful. Castles were strongly built and defended to safeguard the people who lived in them. Within their walls were busy, bustling communities. The owner and his family lived there with the servants and craftspeople who worked for them. Sometimes there was a private army as well, when the lord called upon his loyal knights to help defend his lands.

Castles were built by important people, such as lords and kings or queens. They were not only splendid homes which the owners could show off to their friends, but military bases from which the surrounding lands were defended. The land around a castle was owned by the lord too. Most castles were built between AD1000 and 1500, a period that is called the Middle Ages. In Europe, the Middle East and parts of Asia around this time, large areas of land were owned by a few wealthy people. They often fought each other to win more land or power for themselves.

▲ NOBLE OWNERS
The lord and lady have an excellent view of their impressive castle as they ride through the countryside. They do not need to work for a living like the peasant who is bowing to them. The owners of castles charged rent from the lands they owned nearby. Peasants could pay their rent in money or by giving produce (such as crops or animals) in return for a strip of land to farm and the protection of the castle.

HIGH SOCIETY ▶
In the great age of castles, the land was owned by a few very rich and powerful people. The most important person was the monarch. Then came lords and ladies (nobles) whose importance depended on how rich they were. The monarch and rich nobles gave land to less powerful knights. In exchange, the knights had to promise to be loyal and to provide soldiers in times of war. The most lowly people were the peasants, or villeins, and there were very many of them.

peasants

merchants and soldiers

knights

nobles (lords and ladies)

monarch

◀ UNDER ATTACK!
The high towers and thick walls of the French castle of Pontaudemer Areunoer were attacked during the 1400s. The attackers are climbing ladders but they are easy targets for the defenders who can shoot them or push them away. Castles were built during times of insecurity, so they had to be strongly defended. Some were situated on steep hillsides or at the top of rocky cliffs. Others had a moat (a deep circular ditch, which was sometimes full of water) around the outer walls to make them difficult to attack.

▲ CHANGING ROLES

The Castel Sant'Angelo in Rome, Italy, was not always a castle. It began as a tomb for the Roman emperor Hadrian in the AD130s. Then, in about AD280, another emperor needed to improve the city defences. He changed the tomb into a fortress that ran the length of the city walls. Various popes then gradually converted Sant'Angelo into a castle. There were rooms to live in, courtyards and storerooms, all safe within the defensive walls.

▲ CASTLES AS TOWNS

A map of the Italian city of Tine in the 1600s shows how a castle could grow into a whole town. The castle made people who were living nearby feel safe and there were also jobs to be found there as servants. Sometimes a castle was built within a town that already existed or the castle and town might be built at the same time. The townspeople usually gave the lord of the castle their loyalty and support in battles. Whole towns were often encircled by strong defensive walls like those around the castles.

▲ A PEACETIME COMMUNITY

The scene at a German castle during the 1400s shows how, even in peacetime, there is a lot going on. The castle was always busy as a centre of local trade and business. Activities were organized to please the rich owners. Feasts were held for important visitors from other regions, and entertainment and hunting trips were arranged. Knights entered tournaments to show off their skills, and to give them valuable practice in fighting skills and horsemanship.

▲ LUXURY HOMES

From the 1500s onwards, European countries became more stable and strongly defended homes were not needed any more. The fairytale castle of Neuschwanstein had large windows and luxury fittings, and was much more comfortable than a real castle. It was built in the late 1800s by King Ludwig II of Bavaria.

Castles Around the World

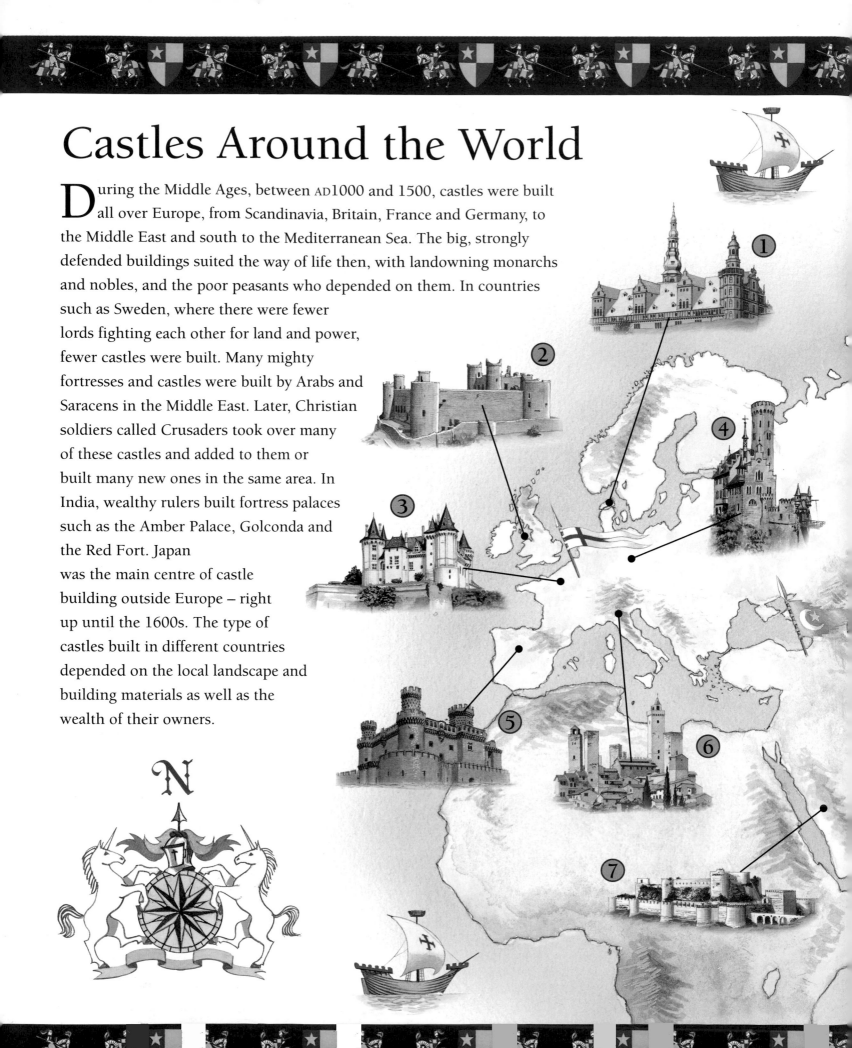

During the Middle Ages, between AD1000 and 1500, castles were built all over Europe, from Scandinavia, Britain, France and Germany, to the Middle East and south to the Mediterranean Sea. The big, strongly defended buildings suited the way of life then, with landowning monarchs and nobles, and the poor peasants who depended on them. In countries such as Sweden, where there were fewer lords fighting each other for land and power, fewer castles were built. Many mighty fortresses and castles were built by Arabs and Saracens in the Middle East. Later, Christian soldiers called Crusaders took over many of these castles and added to them or built many new ones in the same area. In India, wealthy rulers built fortress palaces such as the Amber Palace, Golconda and the Red Fort. Japan was the main centre of castle building outside Europe – right up until the 1600s. The type of castles built in different countries depended on the local landscape and building materials as well as the wealth of their owners.

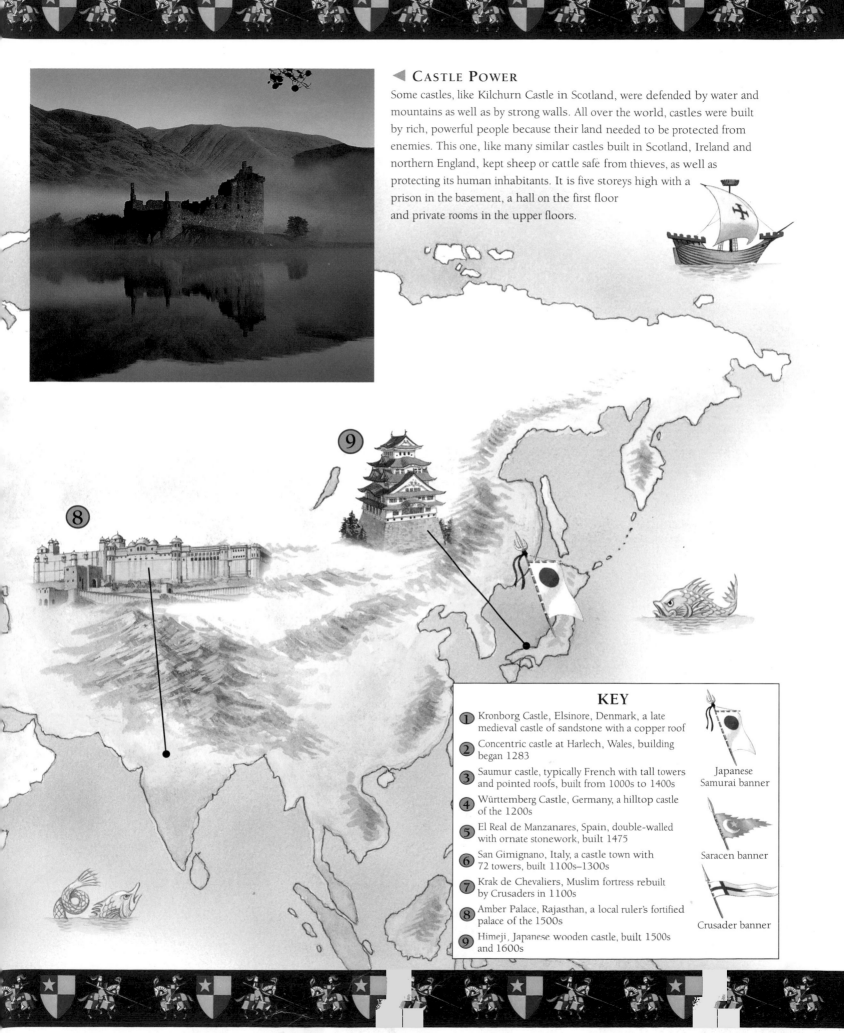

◀ CASTLE POWER

Some castles, like Kilchurn Castle in Scotland, were defended by water and mountains as well as by strong walls. All over the world, castles were built by rich, powerful people because their land needed to be protected from enemies. This one, like many similar castles built in Scotland, Ireland and northern England, kept sheep or cattle safe from thieves, as well as protecting its human inhabitants. It is five storeys high with a prison in the basement, a hall on the first floor and private rooms in the upper floors.

KEY

1. Kronborg Castle, Elsinore, Denmark, a late medieval castle of sandstone with a copper roof
2. Concentric castle at Harlech, Wales, building began 1283
3. Saumur castle, typically French with tall towers and pointed roofs, built from 1000s to 1400s
4. Württemberg Castle, Germany, a hilltop castle of the 1200s
5. El Real de Manzanares, Spain, double-walled with ornate stonework, built 1475
6. San Gimignano, Italy, a castle town with 72 towers, built 1100s–1300s
7. Krak de Chevaliers, Muslim fortress rebuilt by Crusaders in 1100s
8. Amber Palace, Rajasthan, a local ruler's fortified palace of the 1500s
9. Himeji, Japanese wooden castle, built 1500s and 1600s

Japanese Samurai banner

Saracen banner

Crusader banner

Castles Through the Ages

Although the great age of castle building was in the Middle Ages, military forts and fortified palaces have been built since ancient times. Many of their features were adapted and used in castles. About 1000BC, the ancient Greeks built fortified palaces and towns. These citadels had mighty stone walls, towers and outer courtyards for protection. The fortified ruins of Mycenae and Tyrins can still be seen today. Around 2,000 years ago, the Romans built forts with garrisons of soldiers to guard the frontiers of their empire. The wooden fort walls were sometimes plastered to look like stone. A small fort was called a *castella* in Latin (the Roman language), which gave us the word castle.

Early European castles consisted of a motte (a mound of earth) topped by a wooden tower which overlooked a bailey (courtyard). However, as weapons became more powerful and castle communities grew larger, stone replaced wood, and castles became larger, more complicated in design, stronger and more permanent.

▲ **ANCIENT PALACE**
The citadel (fortified palace) of Mycenae stands on a hill overlooking the surrounding countryside. Like later castles, it had strong walls made of huge blocks of stone to protect the people who lived inside. On one side the walls rose sheer from a vertical rockface. A massive gate carved with lions guarded an entrance. Mycenae was built when small, separate kingdoms often fought against each other, rather as the medieval lords did in western Europe.

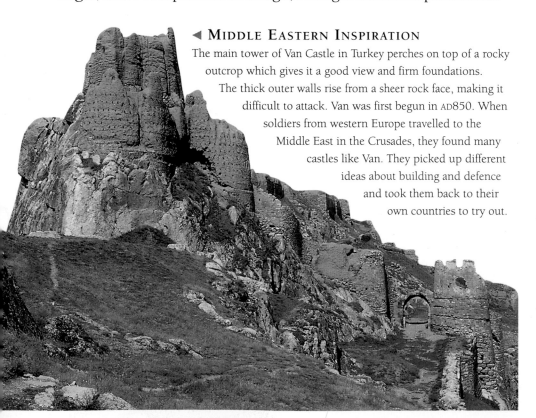

◀ **MIDDLE EASTERN INSPIRATION**
The main tower of Van Castle in Turkey perches on top of a rocky outcrop which gives it a good view and firm foundations. The thick outer walls rise from a sheer rock face, making it difficult to attack. Van was first begun in AD850. When soldiers from western Europe travelled to the Middle East in the Crusades, they found many castles like Van. They picked up different ideas about building and defence and took them back to their own countries to try out.

▲ **STONE STRONGHOLDS**
Defenders had an excellent view of the approaching enemy from the top of Tarascon Castle in southern France. Stone towers, with very thick walls and firm foundations, replaced wooden ones in the early Middle Ages. They are often known as keeps, but in their day were called great towers or donjons. Keeps were arranged like a block of flats, with the upper floors each containing a grand, self-contained living area occupied by the lord of the castle.

▲ ENCLOSED SAFETY

The courtyard of Saumur Castle in France is protected by a high stone wall with towers and a well-defended gatehouse. Courtyard castles began to be built in the 1190s in northern Europe. They relied on strong outer walls with a gatehouse to protect the buildings within the courtyard rather than one great tower or keep. The courtyard well was crucial too. Its large underground water tank provided water even if the castle was besieged and no one could leave to get fresh supplies.

▲ DOUBLE TAKE

The castle of El Real de Manzanares, near Madrid, has double walls. Attackers who broke through the lower, outer walls found themselves trapped between these and the higher inner wall. They were then easy prey for the defenders. Stone double-walled castles were built from the mid-1100s onwards. The idea for them may have come from Christian knights who had seen the twin walls of the city of Constantinople (now called Istanbul) during the Crusades.

◀ JAPANESE TIERS

The main tower of Himeji Castle in Japan rises in a series of tiers, each of which was defended by warriors. Elaborately decorated roofs indicated the owner was of high rank. The greatest age of Japanese castle building came later than Europe's. Himeji began as a small fortress in the Middle Ages but was extended in the 1500s and 1600s by the warlord Ikeda Terumasa. There was a lot of fighting for power between Japanese warlords at this time just as in Europe during the Middle Ages. The main tower was the heart of the castle and contained rooms for the lord, his family and warriors as well as watchtowers and storage areas. The wooden walls were covered in plaster to reduce the risk of fire and were able to withstand earthquakes.

▲ THE END OF CASTLES

Cinderella's Palace at Walt Disney World in Florida, is based on the King of Bavaria's fantasy castle in Neuschwanstein, Germany. Castles like these were not used for defence. By the end of the Middle Ages people did not need to defend their homes because their way of life had changed. Governments had become more stable and had started to trade with each other. People had begun to live more peacefully and settle in towns instead of fortified castles.

Building a Castle

Imagine how difficult it must have been to construct an enormous building like a castle without modern machines, such as cranes and bulldozers. Most of the work had to be carried out by the muscle power of hundreds of workmen who needed to be told what to do. Tools were simple. Masons shaped the stone with mallets and chisels; carpenters used chisels, hammers, saws and planes. There were some machines, such as winches, for lifting heavy materials. These might be operated by a windmill or watermill, but more often were attached to a treadmill. Treadmills are heavy, giant wheels that were turned for power by a man walking inside.

Simple timber and earthwork castles could be built in a few weeks or months but a great stone castle could take a lifetime to complete. They were usually built on a site that needed defending or where many people were already living. Ideally, a castle was built above the surrounding country to make it difficult to attack, and near to food (such as a forest for hunting) and fresh water. Raw materials such as stone, rubble, timber, ropes, sand, iron and lead had to be transported to the site, often over great distances.

▲ A BUILDER'S VIEW

The builder is in a very precarious position. High up on the castle tower there is nothing between him and the ground but fresh air. Far below, fellow workers load fresh supplies of building materials on to ropes and pulleys. Wooden scaffolding was flimsy and bound together with ropes. The poles were made secure by slotting them into holes left unfilled in the wall. These were called puglog holes.

▲ CASTLE DESIGN

A medieval architect explains his plans. Detailed drawings of complicated buildings such as castles and cathedrals had to be made. The architect had to look at the type of land the castle was to be built on, and at local building materials. Design and size of the building also depended on what the castle owners wanted and how much they had to spend.

▲ WEIGHTY PROBLEMS

Workers find solutions to the problems of moving blocks of stone using a simple pulley system and many workers. Stone was the most popular building material in western Europe, brick was more common farther east. Stone was transported by sea or river, rather than by roads which became bogged down and impassable in the rain.

MASTER MASONS ▶

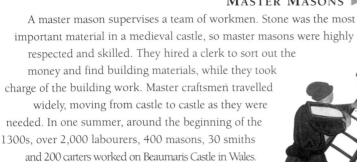

A master mason supervises a team of workmen. Stone was the most important material in a medieval castle, so master masons were highly respected and skilled. They hired a clerk to sort out the money and find building materials, while they took charge of the building work. Master craftsmen travelled widely, moving from castle to castle as they were needed. In one summer, around the beginning of the 1300s, over 2,000 labourers, 400 masons, 30 smiths and 200 carters worked on Beaumaris Castle in Wales.

▲ STONE RECYCLING

An old Roman altar makes a useful door lintel to support the gatehouse doorway at Carlisle Castle, England. It probably predates the castle by about 1,000 years. Stone was expensive and heavy to transport, so existing stones were recycled. When castles were no longer needed, many of them were demolished and sold off piecemeal for building stone.

A LONG-TERM JOB ▶

The king keeps an eye on the castle being built next door. Maybe it was his gift to a favourite nobleman. Many different workmen were involved in castle building. Carpenters sawed wooden beams and built scaffolding. Stone was cut by hewers at the quarry, carted to the building site, then cut and shaped by masons. Limeburners made mortar (a mixture of sand, quicklime and water) to bond the stone together. Tilers worked on the roofing and plumbers fitted lead pipes, while blacksmiths forged and shaped metal for locks, doors and portcullises.

Build to Defend

A castle needed to be big enough for the owner's family, servants and private army, and strong enough to withstand attack. The outer walls of the real life version of this model were high to prevent attackers climbing over them on ladders. This also meant that soldiers inside could look down on to the enemy and have an effective line of fire for their arrows. The stone towers had to be built firmly on solid rock that usually sloped outwards for extra support.

The entrance to a castle is its most vulnerable spot. That is why the model castle's entrance is placed at the top of a flight of steps. In real life, these would have led into a forebuilding on the side of the main tower. Windows at low levels were just narrow slits that attackers would have difficulty climbing into, but from which archers inside the castle could easily fire arrows.

You will need: ruler, pencil, scissors, 4 sheets of A1 (50 x 76cm) stiff cardboard, 19 x 7cm thin card, 50 x 15cm corrugated cardboard, glue, large roll of masking tape, pair of compasses, acrylic paints, firm-bristled artist's paintbrushes.

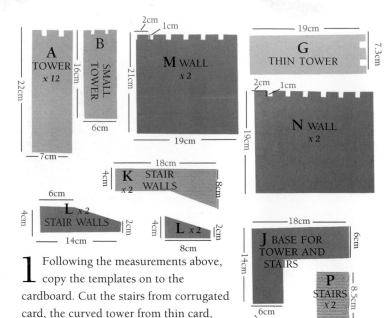

1 Following the measurements above, copy the templates on to the cardboard. Cut the stairs from corrugated card, the curved tower from thin card, and the rest from the thick card.

The great tower (or keep) of Rochester Castle has a tower at each corner like the model castle. It was probably begun about 1088 by King William I. He needed to defend the lands he had conquered in England.

5 Use a pair of compasses to draw a 9.5cm-diameter circle on the thick card. Mark it into quarters. Cut out a quarter for the curved tower floors.

6 Assemble the two right-angled walls I, and the floors of the curved tower in the same way as you made the three square towers.

11 Make the small tower in the same way as you made the other towers. Put two walls in place, then the floors, and finally the third wall.

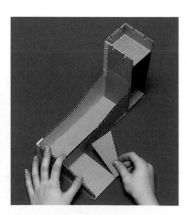

12 Glue the small tower at the end of the long part of the stair base section J. Glue the stair walls K and L into place, as shown above.

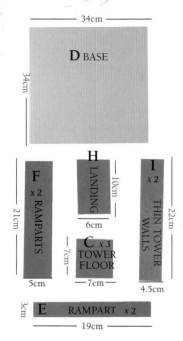

34cm

D BASE

34cm

F
x 2
RAMPARTS
21cm
5cm

H
LANDING
10cm
6cm

C x 3
TOWER
FLOOR
7cm
7cm

I
x 2
THIN TOWER
WALLS
22cm
4.5cm

E RAMPART x 2
3cm
19cm

2 For each of the three square towers, glue two **A** walls together on the tower floor **C**. Then glue the upper floor section **C** in place.

3 For each of the three square towers, glue the open edges of the floor, tower base and standing wall. Then stick the third wall into place.

4 Leave for the glue to dry. Then tape strips of masking tape over all the outside corners of the tower walls. This will neaten and secure the joins.

7 Glue the edges of the thin tower walls **I**, then curve the thin card wall section **G**. Stick it into place. Masking tape over the joins to strengthen and neaten.

8 Place the four completed towers at each corner of the main castle floor **D**. Glue them into position and reinforce the joins with masking tape.

9 Cut the crenellations in the top of the walls **M** and **N**. Glue the bottom and side edges of the four walls. Stick them into position between the towers.

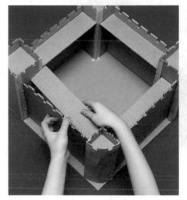

10 Glue the outer and side edges of the rampart pathway sections **E** and **F**. Fit them into place just below the top of the crenellated walls.

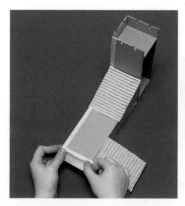

13 Glue the landing section **H** over the bottom end of the stair walls. Stick the corrugated stairs **P** along the slopes. Tape all the joins.

14 Cut out about 30 small, irregular rectangles of thick card, and and glue them in random groups on the outer walls of the castle.

When you have painted the castle and stair-tower and fitted them together, you can paint in some windows. The walls of a real stone keep like this were built of individual stones painstakingly cemented together and were up to 5m thick. Inside there were usually three floors, with passages and stairways linking them.

Reconstructing the Past

Today, most castles are empty and forbidding, with the wind whistling through broken walls and weeds climbing over the ruins. Yet they were once like small towns, full of bustling people, farm animals, dogs, cats, and a host of different noises and smells. The silent remains of stones and mounds of earth are clues to how the castle was once used – if you know how to read them. They can help you piece together the past and bring the castle back to life. What is now a dry, grassy ditch around the outer walls may once have been a moat filled with water to keep enemies at bay. Holes in walls may have been firing points for archers, or for dropping missiles through, or they may simply have supported floor beams. Blackened stones show where fireplaces or ovens once were. The remains of narrow towers may have housed space-saving spiral staircases – the stairs wound up to the right, to make it hard for a right-handed enemy soldier to swing his sword.

When you are exploring a castle ruin, try to imagine what it was once like. That patch of faded plaster on an inside wall may once have been brightly painted or hung with rich tapestries.

▲ WHAT SHAPE ARE THE SLITS?

Look at the shape of the narrow slits in the castle walls. If they are wide in parts, they are probably arrow slits (or loops). The slits are too narrow for the enemy to fire into, but perfect for an archer to fire from. He would also be under cover at the same time. The fishtail shape (*left*) allowed an archer to aim in different directions. Loops cut with circular eye holes called *oillets* were probably for firing crossbows from. The slit on the right with a widened circle is a gun loop for the muzzle of a gun to fit into.

▲ HOW BIG ARE THE HOLES?

Large holes in castle walls were needed for cannons. The guns moved backwards when they were fired and had to be swung round to take aim. Some towers on the outer walls of Dover Castle, England, were demolished to make platforms for firing cannons. This castle in Tripoli, Lebanon, has a large hole in the wall for a cannon.

TOILET FACILITIES ▶

If you see a hump in an outer wall like this, it is probably a former toilet. On the inside was a small room called a garderobe. The toilet might have been covered with a wooden seat, and sometimes there was a washbasin as well. A handful of hay or torn strips of linen took the place of toilet paper, and sweet-smelling herbs were sprinkled on the floor. Shafts from the toilet led into a latrine pit or into the moat. A worker called a gong farmer carried out the unpleasant and unhealthy job of emptying the pit.

WHAT ELSE CAN YOU SEE? ▶

If you see up-and-down battlements like these on the top of castle walls, imagine being a soldier standing behind them. They were not just there for decoration, but acted like shields of stone with gaps between them. Soldiers could fire at enemies through the gaps (crenels) and hide behind the shields (merlons). This meant they could fire down on enemies while still remaining under cover. Brick is the main building material of this castle, which is a clue that it is younger than a stone-built one. As life became calmer, people began to build homes that were more like country houses and did not have to be so heavily fortified. The wide pointed arch shape of the big windows at the bottom of the picture is also a clue to age. This style came after the rounded arches of the Norman castles and the more pointed arches of the earlier Middle Ages. This castle is Tattershall, built in about 1440.

▲ FLOOR CLUES

The 38m tower at Rochester Castle, England, originally had several wooden floors, which have now rotted away. You can see the lines of holes in the walls that held the wooden beams that supported the floor above. Another way of telling where a floor or a roof used to be is to look for stone blocks called corbels sticking out of the wall. These also supported wooden beams.

MISSILES AWAY! ▶

Sticking out from the tops of some castle walls are stone parapets resting on stone brackets (corbels). The space between each pair of corbels is called a machicolation. These were like specially built missile chutes. Objects such as stones, pitch, boiling water or quicklime could be dropped on the attackers standing below. Quicklime burned the skin of the enemy soldiers and stones dropped from a great height had a strong striking force by the time they reached the ground. Death would be painful this way.

Who Lived in Castles?

The most important people in a castle were the lord and lady and their family. A lord often had several castles on his lands and stayed at each one in turn. Wherever he went, a large group of his followers and servants travelled with him. When the lord was away, other servants stayed and kept the castle going. They repaired and cleaned the building, grew, harvested and preserved food, did the washing and looked after the animals. Peasant servants who worked in the kitchens or with the animals were the least important people in the castle. Some servants, such as those who waited on the lord and lady, were of gentle birth, and apart from the ladies-in-waiting, most were usually young, male, and fit to fight. Stewards looked after the castle's finances and supplies. Reeves and bailiffs managed the lord's farms and collected rents. The marshal decided who lived or stayed in which rooms. A total household of 100 people or so was quite usual.

▲ **REFRESHMENT**
A female servant gives some wine to a male groom. The grooms looked after the lord's and lady's favourite horses as well as the heavier horses ridden in battle. Most people who worked in castles were men. Their wives may have had jobs in the kitchens, as laundry maids, or as ale wives in the brewhouse. Laundry maids cleaned dirty clothes and seamstresses repaired any tears or holes.

▲ **DRESSING TO IMPRESS**
A lady needs help from a maid to put on her complicated hat. First the maid has to braid the lady's long hair and bind it in a length of cloth so that not a hair is out of place. This steeple hat is held in shape by a wire frame. The maid fixes it on firmly so that it will not be knocked off in the narrow passages. Some hats worn in medieval times were 1m tall.

FAMILY ROOMS ▶
The lord's family had private rooms, usually in a high part of the castle. Some families kept pet animals, like this one with a dog and a monkey. Every lord wanted to have children to inherit his castle and lands. Because of poor hygiene and medicines, about half the children died before they were 15 years old.

▲ CASTLE LOVERS

In a sheltered garden, a nobleman tells a lady of his love for her. He may be the son and heir of the castle, and she may be visiting from another family. When they were six or seven years old, children were often sent to live in another castle. The girls became maids and learned about the duties of a lady, the boys were pages and learned the lord's business. It was also a chance to meet other families. Most girls were married by the age of 14 years. Their parents arranged for them to marry a man from a suitable family. Everything a woman owned became her husband's when she married. Knights and nobles often married women for their land and wealth.

FIGHTING PRESENCE ▶

A knight arrives at the castle ready to protect the lord. In peacetime, only a few soldiers guarded a castle. They were called the garrison, and were probably a combination of knights and local soldiers. In the early days of the Middle Ages, knights lived permanently in the castle and protected the lord when he moved from one estate to another. Later, knights began to have their own estates. Then, they only stayed at the lord's castle when an attack was expected. From the 1300s, lords began to hire soldiers from outside. These soldiers fought for money rather than from a sense of loyalty to the lord.

◀ LADY IN CHARGE

When her husband is away, the lady has to greet and entertain visitors to the castle. In this picture, the Countess of Boulogne is welcoming the Count of Artois in the 1400s. It was important for powerful people to entertain their friends in case they needed their support in times of war. Ladies also ran the castle business when their husbands were away and if the castle was attacked, they even had to organize its defence. If the husband died in battle, the firstborn son took over.

▲ SOLDIER RULERS

A member of the Tokugawa family rides from the gate of Nijo Castle in the Japanese city of Kyoto. In the early 1600s (known as the Tokugawa period) this castle was home to the family of one of Japan's great soldier-rulers, Tokugawa Ieyasu. As well as the family, a garrison of soldiers lived there. The castle was a centre of trade, law and learning for the whole area, so teachers, lawyers, businessmen and craftworkers lived there too.

High Fashion

If you are having a bad-hair day, you could do what ladies did in the Middle Ages – hide your hair beneath a fancy headdress. This ring-shaped chaplet is one of the more simple headdress styles worn in medieval times. The more wealthy, fashionable and important a lady was, the more elaborate her clothes were. Some robes were embroidered and trimmed with fur – they were extremely expensive and expected to last a lifetime. There were no shops in which to buy readymade clothes, so traders came to the castle to present a choice of materials and designs. When the lady had chosen, tailors made the clothes.

You will need: scissors, 30 x 4cm strip corrugated cardboard, masking tape, 2m fine fabric, about 3-4m netting, two round bath sponges about 10cm diameter, string, watercolour paint and brush, coloured nylon stocking or tights, cotton wool or stuffing, coloured wrapping tapes or ribbons, needle and thread, 1m gold braid, glue, 2 x 2cm silver card, 3 x 7cm lengths thin wire, beads.

Fashions of the 1100s and 1200s reveal rich fabrics, fantastic hats and pointed shoes. Some ladies' headdresses looked like animal horns or butterfly wings. Others were tall and pointed with long pieces of fine flowing cloth hanging down the back. A lady in medieval clothes could not easily hurry from place to place, even if the castle was on fire or being attacked.

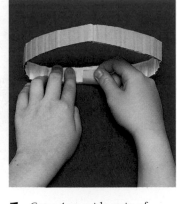

1 Cut a 4cm-wide strip of corrugated card (about 30cm) in a circle or to fit around your head exactly. Overlap the ends and tape them together.

2 Cut two squares of fabric, each one big enough to wrap around a sponge. Cut two squares of netting slightly larger than the fabric squares.

4 Paint the card head circle. Thread two lengths of string through each sponge and net ball. Use the string to hang one on each side of the circlet.

5 Cut the bottom half leg off a stocking or pair of tights. Pack tightly with stuffing to make a firm, full sausage shape. Knot the open end to close it.

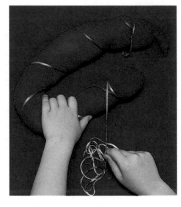

6 Tie the ribbon around one end of the sausage. Wind it diagonally along the sausage. Wind it back again to cross diagonally over the first row.

steeple hat or hennin

butterfly headdresses

steeple hat or hennin

9 Cut out a flower shape from the silver card as shown. Bend one end of the wire into a hook. Thread some beads on the other end. Then bend this over.

3 Lay the fabric squares over the net squares. Place a sponge in the middle of each. Gather the fabrics over the sponge. Tie with string.

A MEDIEVAL GOWN

1 Sew one row of running stitches along one side of the fabric, with the thread knotted at one end and left free at the other.

2 Pull the free thread to gather the fabric until the material is the right length to go around your chest. Tie the threads securely.

3 Glue the braid over the gathered edge of the fabric. Leave enough free at the back to tie a bow. Wear the skirt over your t-shirt.

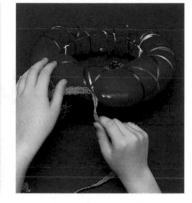

7 Thread ribbon through the ribbon crossovers on the sausage. Then take it over and around the head circlet to join the sausage and band together.

8 Sew the two ends of the sausage together. Sew one end of the gold braid to cover the join. Then glue the braid around the sausage, as shown.

Ring padded with dried plant stalks or another lightweight material

Coiled braids of hair

A real medieval hat like this was called a chaplet. It was made of silk or satin and held in place by a hair net. The ring-shaped chaplet fitted on top of a veil, and the veil hung down at the back of the head just like the one in the picture. Ladies often shaved their hair at the front so that no hair would show and their foreheads would look high. However this is not a good idea for you as it is dangerous and would not look at all fashionable! For an authentic medieval look, you could just tuck your hair out of sight under the hat instead.

10 Glue the flower shape on the front of the head-dress. Hook the wired beads in the middle. Glue more beads and braids around the headdress.

11 Make a double pleat in the remaining length of fabric to make the veil. Fix to the inside back half of the headdress with tape.

Everyday Life

Life in a castle was always busy. The cooks woke early to provide food for all the people in the castle. They lit fires using firewood cut from the nearby forests and drew water from the well. Everyone drank beer (ale) with their meals, so there was also a busy brewhouse. The lower servants tended the poultry, pigs, cattle, goats and horses that lived within the castle grounds. Gardeners grew vegetables and herbs. Carpenters and masons carried out repair work. Soldiers and horses trained constantly so they would be ready for the next fight.

The castle was a business centre, bank and town hall. Peasants came to pay their rent, to have their corn ground in the lord's mills or their bread baked in castle ovens. Their problems were often sorted out by the castle steward and other officials. On market days, the courtyard swarmed with people from the castle and its lands and rang with the cries of farmers and traders.

▲ METAL WORKING

The castle blacksmith was in constant demand. He made weapons and horseshoes for the knights, pots for the cooks and even sewing thimbles for the ladies. His tools were little different from those of today. Nails and hoops for barrels were hammered flat on an anvil, tongs held hot metal over the furnace, snips were used for cutting sheets of metal. The blacksmith's workshop was away from the main castle to reduce the risk of fire.

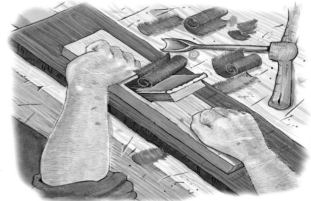

▲ CLEVER HANDS

Yet another plank to plane smooth! A castle carpenter's job is never done. The roof and ceiling beams are rotting from the damp and woodworm. The lord wants new panelling in the Great Hall, and the cook needs a wooden platter. The carpenter uses tools similar to those used today. The one on the bench is a gouge auger to dig out holes in wooden surfaces.

January

February

March

April

May

August

September

October

A PEASANT'S YEAR

Life for the peasants was an endless round of hard work. In return for a strip of land to farm, they had to look after the lord's fields. The castle depended on them for food. In winter, the ground was prepared, and the animals were slaughtered then preserved by salting or smoking. In spring, newborn animals were tended and the fruit trees pruned. Then came harvesting and sowing crops ready for the next year.

LADY'S LEISURE ▶

The lady has several ladies-in-waiting. They not only wait on her hand and foot, but clean her rooms, and probably weave clothes for the entire castle community, too. Ladies-in-waiting were usually of noble birth, and were sometimes relations. The lady herself had to learn to manage the household, and to give instructions to traders and servants. However, in her free time, she could work at her embroidery, play music, sing, or perhaps write a poem. Then she might call in a storyteller or a jester to entertain her.

◀ BE PREPARED!

In the armoury, weapons and armour are kept in constant readiness for action. The metal must be oiled and polished to keep it from rusting. Armour was rolled around in a barrel of sand to scour off rust. A suit of armour cost about the same as a car would cost today, so dents had to be hammered out and holes sealed. Hammerers and polishers made steel plates which locksmiths then joined together with hinges. Helmets were made by the master armourer and decorated by engravers. An armoury was often in the castle grounds, in a courtyard building or the basement of a tower. Sometimes, the castle used the armoury in a nearby town or village.

Ioan. Stradanus invent.   Ioan. Collaert sculp.   Phls Galle excud.

June

July

November

December

HANDY CONTAINERS ▶

These two coopers (barrel-makers) had a vital part to play in the everyday life of the castle. Barrels were filled with wine, beer, cider, salted meat and other food. People washed clothes in them and dyed clothes too. All master craftworkers, such as coopers, smiths and carpenters, taught their skills to young apprentices over many years

Sew for the Castle

Most girls and women were taught to spin and sew. Making small items, like this medieval-style needlework design to decorate a cushion cover, was a popular pastime. Tapestries were much bigger and usually made by weavers. They were hung on the walls of important rooms, such as the Great Hall.

Before any needlework could begin, the canvas background had to be woven, and the yarns spun and dyed. There were no factories with machines for making cloth, or shops where you could buy lengths of fabric. Wool for spinning needlepoint yarn or weaving into cloth came from the sheep on the lord's estate. Linen for fine embroidery and cloth came from flax plants grown in the fields.

The short fibres were spun into lengths of yarn on hand-held spindles at first. Then, in the early 1300s, spinning wheels were invented. Even today, unmarried women are sometimes called spinsters, the name given to women who spun thread. Cloth was coloured by soaking it in a tub filled with natural dyes made from plant roots or leaves.

You will need: black pen, soft leaded pencil, 8 x 9cm square of tracing paper, 15cm square of white linen, adhesive tape, scissors, red, green, blue and orange, double-stranded embroidery threads, large-eyed needle, ruler.

The women of the castle set about one of their main tasks – making cloth for clothes, bedlinen and drapes. To prepare wool for a weaving loom, it first had to be washed. Then, to remove the tangles, it was pulled between two spiked pads. This is called carding the wool – look in the bottom right-hand corner of the picture to see the woman doing the carding. Finally, the wool was woven into cloth on a loom.

1 Use a pen to copy the design (Step 9) on to the tracing paper. Turn the paper over. Trace over the motif outline with the soft-leaded pencil.

2 Tape the tracing, pencilled side down, on the square of fabric. Trace over the motif again, so that the pencilled image transfers on to the fabric.

4 Start with the scroll shape at the bottom of the design. Push the needle from the back of the fabric to the front. Pull the thread through.

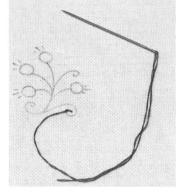

5 Push the needle through the fabric about 2mm along the line of the scroll. Pull the thread through half way along the first stitch (see box top right).

9 Thread the needle with a length of the blue thread. Sew a single stitch for the short details on the flowers, and two stitches for the middle ones.

3 Cut a long piece of the orange double-stranded embroidery thread. Thread the needle. Knot the ends of the thread with a double knot.

STEM STITCH FOCUS

1 Bring the thread from back to front. Hold the end of the thread at the back.

2 Without pulling the end through, push the thread into the fabric farther along.

3 Take the thread to run alongside the first stitch. Sew over the loose end at the back.

4 Pull the thread back through just beyond the first stitch, and continue diagonally. If you take the thread over the loose end at the back as you sew, this is a way of sewing your stitches without having to tie a knot.

6 Carefully continue your stem stitch all the way along the scroll. The stitches should overlap so that they make a continuous, even line.

7 Thread the needle with another length of embroidery thread. Start at the base of the stems and sew along them in the same way.

8 To sew the flowerheads, thread the needle with a length of the red embroidery thread. Sew the stem stitch in a circle.

In medieval times, it was only the girls who were taught to sew, the boys had to learn other skills. Decorative embroidery was mainly done by noblewomen. Peasant women could not afford the time or the materials. Samplers were made to show a range of different stitches and how they were done. Making this needlework will help you to practise your sewing. If you sew your name and the date on it as well, people in the future will know when it was made and who did the sewing.

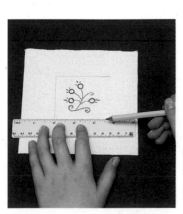

10 Use a pencil and ruler to mark points 1cm from the edges of the motif. Rule light pencil lines between the pointsto draw a border.

11 You can use the single design to decorate something small, like a purse. You can repeat the motif on a larger piece of fabric, as shown.

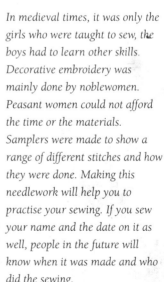

Food and Feasting

Imagine eating roast peacock or heron from a gold or silver plate, or a wild boar's head or an enormous fish being set in front of you. This was the sort of food that was served on special occasions at the castle banquet. Formal meals were a way of showing off the wealth of the castle owner. Eating began at about 10 or 11 o'clock in the morning and could last for hours. All the food came from the castle lands – fruit from orchards and vineyards, grain for bread from the fields, game such as venison, hare and pheasant hunted from the forests, and fish from the rivers and lakes.

By the time the food reached the table in the banqueting hall, it was often cool. The kitchen was usually across the courtyard from the main castle buildings because of the fear of fire. Sometimes passages were built so the food could be carried to the banqueting hall under cover.

Peasants and servants were not invited to castle feasts. They ate simple meals, mainly bread and pottage (thick soup), with a little bacon, milk, cheese and butter. There were no refrigerators or freezers to keep food fresh. Food was preserved by salting, smoking, pickling and drying.

▲ THE OX ROAST

It takes sweat, muscle power and several days to spit-roast an ox. The animal carcases were fixed to a long pole. They had to be turned constantly over spitting flames, to make sure they were cooked. Dripping fat was collected to be spread on bread. Meat was served with thick sauces, strongly flavoured with herbs or spices which helped to disguise the taste of meat if it had begun to go bad. Spices came from distant countries, and only the wealthy could afford them.

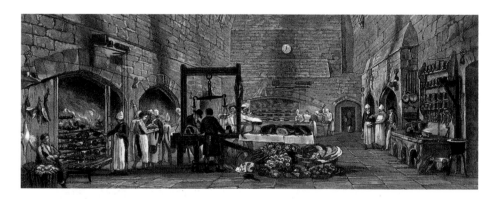

◀ DAILY BREAD

The baker shovels batch after batch of bread from the furnace-like oven. There is bread to be baked every day. He has stripped to the waist because he is so hot, and uses a peel (a long wooden shovel) to move the loaves in the oven. Castles sometimes had their own windmills to grind wheat into flour. Peasants who lived on the castle lands often brought bread to be baked in the big castle ovens.

▲ COOKING BIG TIME

The fire and cooking range in a castle burned all year round in the vast kitchens. Some kitchens were so big there was enough space to roast three whole oxen. Apart from roasting over the fire, big cauldrons (pots) were hung on chains above the flames. Different types of food were cooked in these, such as joints of ham, vegetables or stew.

RICH PICKINGS

Under the banquet table is a good place to be for the castle cats and dogs. They have to fight with the resident rats and mice for the best scraps. It was not considered good manners to feed dogs from the table, but leftover bones and scraps of food were usually tossed on the floor. People also spat on the floor (this was considered polite) which quickly became dirty and was not cleaned very often. The dirt attracted rats and mice, which then spread germs and disease.

BELOW THE SALT

The tables set away from the king are packed with people who are less important than the nobles at the top of the table. These less important people were said to be sitting "below the salt". Salt was placed only before the king or lord and his family who sat "above the salt". This was because salt was expensive since it was mined in distant places and had to be bought from travelling merchants. It was not used in cooking because it was so precious.

FRESH AIR FEASTING ►

Castle noblemen enjoy a picnic in the forest before a day's hunting. They need to build up their energy because the hunt will be long, hard and tiring. Lords and ladies ate a great deal of meat and especially liked game (hunted) animals, such as pheasant, partridge, deer and hare. The picnic food would have included game pies, cakes and wine. Even at a picnic in the open air, the lord is still sitting at a top table to make sure everyone remembers that he is the most important person there.

Sweet and Savoury

It was quite usual to have a mixture of sweet and savoury dishes in one course at a castle feast. This flan mixes savoury cheese with sugar and spice all in one dish. The pinch of saffron makes the cream cheese mixture a rich colour. In medieval times, food was often coloured with vegetable dyes such as saffron and sandalwood or sometimes even gold. Saffron was very expensive, as it comes only from the flowers of a type of Mediterranean crocus. Even today it is bought in tiny quantities. For hundreds of years, it was a sign of wealth and status. Other sweet pies might have been made with cream, eggs, dates and prunes. Do remember to wash and clear up when you have finished cooking. Before the days of dishwashers and washing up liquid, pots and pans were scoured clean with sand and soapy herbs.

You will need: two large eggs, pinch of saffron, hot water, 170g cream cheese, tablespoon of caster sugar, teaspoon of powdered ginger, pinch of salt, pack of readymade shortcrust pastry (about 250g). Measuring scales, teaspoon, tablespoon, two mixing bowls, four small dishes, plate, egg cup, measuring scales, tea strainer, fork, whisk, spoon, flour, pastry board, rolling pin, greased butter paper, flan tin about 15cm diameter, knife.

A lord enjoys eating his food from splendid silver and gold dishes, and drinks from a pewter or silver chalice. He might also have used wooden plates, but lowlier people did not have plates at all. They ate from trenchers (large pieces of coarse brown bread). The trenchers soaked up grease and sauces from the food and could be eaten afterwards. Even at the top table, people ate with their fingers, or with spoons. They carried their own knives with them. Forks were not invented until the 1500s. However, food was cut into small pieces so it could be easily stabbed with a knife. It was also soft and mushy so it could be scooped up on to the bread. After a meal, a servant called an ewerer brought water for the lord to wash his fingers.

1 Have all your bowls and utensils laid out ready to use. Measure all the ingredients carefully. Place them in separate bowls on the working surface.

2 Break each egg in turn on to a plate. Place an egg cup over the yolk. Tip the plate over a bowl so that the white pours away. Put the yolk in to a bowl.

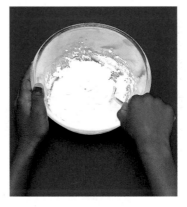

4 Use a metal fork or spoon to mash the cream cheese. Carry on blending until there are no lumps and the cheese is of a soft and creamy consistency.

5 Add the tablespoonful of caster sugar to the egg yolks. Use a whisk to beat the egg and sugar together until the mixture has thickened a little.

9 Roll the pastry circle around the rolling pin. Pick it up and hold it just above the flan dish. Unroll the pastry carefully to fall gently in to the flan tin.

3 Put the saffron in a bowl. Heat some water and pour a little of it over the saffron. Leave until the water turns golden and then strain into another bowl.

Youths from other noble families serve at a feast in the Great Hall. In this way, they learned good manners, polished speech, and how to behave. At some castles, a taster tried out food before it was served to the noble or royal family, to make sure that it was not poisoned.

6 Gradually add the softened cheese to the egg mixture. Use the whisk to gently beat in the cheese until it has completely blended with the egg mixture.

7 Add the ginger, salt and saffron water to the mixture. Stir in all the ingredients lightly. Preheat the oven to 200°C (400°F) or Gas Mark 6-7.

8 Roll the pastry on a lightly floured board. Make it slightly larger than the flan tin and about 5mm thick. Lightly grease the tin with butter paper.

10 Use your fingertips to press the pastry into the edges of the flan tin. Trim any overlapping edges of pastry with a knife.

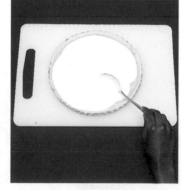

11 Spoon the cream cheese mixture into the pastry base, then place the flan in the centre of the preheated oven and bake for 20–25 minutes.

Sweet cheese flan was one of the earliest known sweet puddings. Cheese was a way of making butter last longer. Another favourite was "Poor Knight's Pudding." This was bread flavoured with sugar and sherry, then dipped in egg yolks and fried in batter.

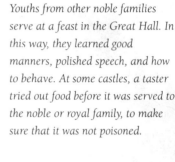

Entertainment

Castle dwellers did not have television, stereos, or discos to keep them amused in their spare time. Instead, people made their own entertainment. They played board games or ball games, danced, wrestled, watched puppet shows and jugglers and listened to storytellers, poets or musicians. Rich lords often employed their own full-time minstrels to play music, and jesters to tell jokes and sing songs. Most entertainers, however, travelled from one castle or town to another. Sometimes, unusual animals such as bears drew crowds of curious onlookers.

Hunting and hawking were probably the most popular pastimes for noble people. They also provided food. Dogs chased prey during a hunt, and tame birds of prey, such as hawks and kestrels, were trained to swoop down and catch smaller birds. The most exciting entertainments were tournaments, when people watched knights in armour on horseback, practising their fighting skills.

▲ PLAYING SOLDIERS

Two friends pull strings to make the toy soldiers fight. Toys were rare. Most seem to have been for boys, and were usually something to do with war or fighting, such as knights on foot or horseback. Young children flew kites or ran with windmills. There were also marbles and pegtops to play with. Indoor games such as Blind Man's Buff and Piggy in the Ring were favourites. The rules of other games, such as hand-in-and-hand-out, remain a mystery.

BALL GAMES ▲

Castle workers play a form of hockey called bandyball. In the 1400s, curved sticks were used to hit a ball, which was larger than a modern hockey ball and probably made of leather. There was also a rough sport similar to football (soccer). In a game like tennis, the palm of the hand was used to hit the ball. The Arabic word for the palm of the hand is *rahat*, which may be where the word racket comes from.

◄ BOARD GAMES

There may be more to this game of chess being played between the 1300s and 1400s than simple fun. Chess was popular with knights because it was a war game. It was played in the Middle East and India and may have been brought back to Europe by the crusading knights on their return home. Chesspieces were often made of bone or ivory and were beautifully carved. Other board games played in castles included draughts, dice and backgammon.

◄ THE THRILL OF THE HUNT

German nobles meet for a big day of hunting and shooting. This is a deer hunt, but foxes, wolves, otters and wild boar were also hunted. Hounds (hunting dogs) were carefully trained and very valuable. They were kept in kennels, cared for by grooms and fed tasty morsels from the animals they helped to catch. Noble people often had a favourite hound that followed them about their castles and lands. Ordinary people were not allowed to catch wild animals on the lord's estates, but many disobeyed the rules and went poaching. If peasants were caught poaching game, they might be blinded or

◄ MUSIC ON HIGH

A drum beats time for the dancers, while the gentle notes of harps and flutes provide the melody. Other instruments might include bagpipes and hurdy-gurdies – which were played by turning a handle. Throughout the golden age of castles, dancing was an important and popular pastime. In a common dance of the 1100s, the dancers wove in and out along a line or circle in time to the music. Later, there were more dances which involved couples.

WANDERING MINSTRELS ►

Poet minstrels sing of love and heroic deeds for the lord and lady of the castle. To please important people, medieval minstrels often composed long poems especially for them. These told of the greatness of their family and ancestors. Minstrels were professional entertainers. In France during the 1100s, many ballads were composed by troubadours, who were amateurs of noble birth.

WILD PARTYING ►

A crocodile and a monkey join the actors, jesters and musicians to entertain the guests at a riotous party. Animals from newly discovered tropical lands during the 1500s were great curiosities for people in Europe. Mummers (actors) were more traditional entertainers. They were local people in disguise who danced or performed plays in exchange for food, drink or money. It was considered unlucky to send them away.

Playing the Fool

See if you can entertain your family like the castle jesters used to do. Noble families often employed jesters full-time, so that they could be cheered up whenever they wanted. It was rather like having their own private comedy act. Jesters dressed in silly costumes with bells and played the fool. However, they were often skilled jugglers and tumblers (acrobats) too. They sang songs and told funny stories and jokes, which were sometimes very rude. They often made fun of the people watching them, and were great at passing on top secret gossip that no one else would dare mention.

You will need: pencil, 24 x 19cm yellow card, tennis ball sized polystyrene ball, 40cm length of 1cm diameter dowel, scissors, glue, red, pink, brown, white and blue acrylic paints, artist's paintbrush, 45cm lengths of yellow and red ribbon, bells, three colourful juggling balls.

The jester's funny, colourful outfit made fun of the fashionable clothes worn by the noble people. To make the costume look even more fun, strands of brightly coloured cloth dangled from the tunic and sleeves. Points, or pretend ears, were made to stick out of the top of the jester's hat.

A JESTER'S STICK

1 Use a pencil to copy the hat shape as shown, on the piece of yellow card. Draw around the ball to make sure the curve at the bottom is the same diameter.

2 Cut out the hat. Put a strip of glue around half of the centre line of the ball. Fit the hat on the glued strip and hold it until it is firmly in place.

TWO-BALL JUGGLE

1 Put a ball in each hand. Throw both of the balls up in the air together in straight lines, and catch them when they fall. This is the easy bit!

2 Throw both balls up together so they cross in front of you. The trick is to make sure they do not bump into each other. Catch each ball in the opposite hand.

3 Now try throwing both balls up together in straight lines again. However, this time, cross your hands over to catch the balls as they fall.

THREE-BALL JUGGLE

1 Hold two balls, 1 and 3, in the right hand (if this is the hand you throw with first). Hold the other ball (2) in the left hand. Stand firm but relaxed.

2 Throw ball 1 up and diagonally across your body. Just as this is starting to drop, throw ball 2 diagonally across from the left hand.

3 Catch ball 1 in your left hand. Just as ball 2 is starting to drop, throw ball 3 up and diagonally across your body towards your left hand.

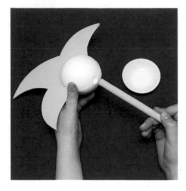

3 Use the pointed end of the scissors to make a hole in the bottom of the ball. Fill the hole with glue and insert the dowelling stick.

4 Paint the stick bright red. When it is dry, paint eyes, mouth, cheeks and hair on the head to make a cheerful face. Paint half of the hat red.

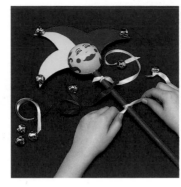

5 Glue bells to the corners of the hat. Then tie bells to lengths of coloured ribbon. Tie the ribbons around the stick, using a simple knot to secure.

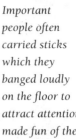

Important people often carried sticks which they banged loudly on the floor to attract attention. The jester's small stick made fun of these. The real sticks usually had serious carved heads on the top. However, the jester's version had a silly head which he banged on the floor as part of his act. The head was sometimes a small version of his own head. The jester sometimes put an animal's bladder on a stick, to make what was called a slapstick. Today, people use the word slapstick to describe a lively knockabout comedy.

4 Throw the right ball diagonally across your body. Just as it is about to drop, throw the left ball diagonally, towards your right hand.

5 Catch the first ball in your left hand but keep your eye on the other ball still in the air. Catch this one in your right hand. Practise until perfect!

Once you have mastered how to juggle, try to make your act even more entertaining. You can pull funny faces as you juggle, or make strange noises. You may even become good enough to tell a joke at the same time as you juggle!

Professional jesters and jugglers who were not employed full-time by one family travelled around. They went from castle to castle and often performed at village fairs. They did not charge much for their entertainment – perhaps a penny – so that poor people could enjoy watching their skills as well.

4 Catch ball 2 in your right hand. Keep your eye on ball 3, the one you threw last. Try not to look at your hands when you catch the balls!

5 Catch the final ball (3) in your left hand. Now you have completed your first juggle. Keep the balls moving in a rhythmical circle.

Inside the Castle Walls

Beyond the seemingly impenetrable walls of a big castle lies a miniature world. This picture is based on Goodrich Castle, on the borders of England and Wales, when it was at its peak in the early 1400s. Like many castles, Goodrich grew gradually, as the wealth and needs of its various owners changed. It started as a simple Norman keep in the mid-1100s. Successive owners added the four great towers which provided living quarters and storerooms for the growing castle community. There are three halls for banqueting, business, and extra living accommodation. A gatehouse and barbican provided double security. They guarded the only approach to the castle along a narrow causeway over a deep ditch.

◀ PRIVATE CHAMBERS

The lord and lady have the rooms with the richest furnishings. Tapestries hang on the walls, and their windows have glass in them (most rooms had oiled cloth or wooden shutters). The tester (four-poster) bed has a canopy to keep dust and insects from falling on the people sleeping below.

THE GATEHOUSE ▶

If the enemy reached the gatehouse, it was uncomfortably close. The soldiers have set aside their longbows for long-distance fire. They can aim their crossbows through the narrow windows while keeping under cover.

▲ THE CHAPEL

The lord and lady have a service in their own private chapel. The chalice (cup) that the priest is holding contains the communion wine. It will be put away safely in the aumbry (cupboard).

▲ THE GREAT HALL

The castle owner doles out a punishment to a prisoner. The Great Hall was where the castle met the outside world. Here, important guests were feasted and business affairs were often conducted. Peasants might come to pay their rents, and traders to display their goods.

KEY

1 kitchen	10 drawbridge
2 living areas and storerooms	11 stepped ramp to gatehouse
3 stables	12 barbican
4 great hall	13 guard chamber
5 owner's living area	14 garderobe
6 keep	15 dry moat
7 hall	16 rocky foundation
8 chapel	17 dungeon
9 gatehouse	

Religious Life

If you were the owner of a castle in medieval times, you would probably have your own private chapel and visit it every day. Religion was a very important part of everyday life during the Middle Ages, as it helped to explain events that people did not understand in the world around them. Disasters such as storms, disease and famine were thought to be punishments from God. People believed that such punishments would not happen if they prayed and performed good deeds. The Church and the priests became very powerful and it was important to keep on the right side of them. Ordinary people went on pilgrimages to holy places such as Canterbury, in England, or Jerusalem. There were many religious festivals when everyone took a holiday (or holy day) and travelling actors performed religious plays. At various times in the 1100s and 1200s, Christians from all over Europe, including peasants, knights and sometimes even children, gathered into armies. They marched or sailed to the Holy Land in Palestine to fight Muslim armies for control of sacred sites. These events were known as the Crusades and the people who took part in them were called Crusaders (soldiers of the cross).

▲ **PRECIOUS ORNAMENTS**

A chalice (cup) and plate of the 1160s, made of silver and gold, were used in church services. In castle chapels, altar ornaments like these showed how much wealthy people were prepared to spend in the interests of religion. Castle families also often employed several priests. The Christian Church itself was very rich and powerful, and had many castles of its own in Europe.

▲ **CRUSADING SPIRIT**

Mighty castles like Krak des Chevaliers (castle of the knights) in Syria were built as fortresses by Muslim soldiers. Then during the Crusades, many were taken over by Christian knights. The Knights Hospitaller – military monks who fought to protect Crusaders and pilgrims visiting the Holy Land – held Krak and defended it against Muslim attack from 1142 to 1271. The fortress had a double ring of defensive walls and a narrow entrance. Inside, the monks built a monastery, enormous granaries to store food, and a windmill.

HIGH CHURCH ►

The chapel that was built in the keep of Dover Castle, England, in the 1180s, is simple in its design. Other castle chapels had stone statues, wall paintings and stained-glass windows. The chapel was often the highest room in a castle so that it was as close as possible to heaven. Some castles also had a large chapel in the courtyard for more lowly castle residents.

LEARNED NUN ▶

The French nun Christine de Pisan, who was born in 1364, sits at her desk. Monks and nuns were among the few who could read and write during the Middle Ages. Some nobles could read, but not many could write. Christine, however, started to write so that she could support herself and her family. She wrote about heroic and virtuous women, as well as about the life of Charles V of France. She also wrote books on history and philosophy, and love poetry. It was not until 1415, when she was about 50 years old, that she decided to become a nun.

▲ LEARN FROM PICTURES

Ceramic tiles like these decorated the floor of many a church and chapel. Some were decorated with the coats of arms of the noble families who owned the chapel, others had floral or abstract patterns. Many chapel decorations – on tiles, stained-glass windows or wood carvings – illustrated characters, scenes and stories from the Bible. In medieval times most people could not read and write. The pictures helped them understand the teachings of the Bible.

AFTER CARE ▶

The grand tomb of Catherine Parr, the sixth and last wife of King Henry VIII of England, is fitting for a noblewoman who was also very religious. It is in Sudeley Castle, for after Henry's death, Catherine married Lord Seymour of Sudeley. She died in 1548. Noble people usually had family tombs in the chapels of their castles. Some tombs, like this one, had life-sized sculptures of the person who had died. Priests and monks were paid to visit the tombs after the burial to pray for the souls of the dead.

Illuminating Letters

Before printing was invented in the 1400s, the only way to have more than one book or manuscript was to copy it out by hand. This made books very valuable and rare. The pages were often beautifully illustrated, with decorated letters like the one in this project. Many noble households had only one book, which in Christian countries was the Bible. Most books were kept in monastery libraries. Much of what we know about life in the past comes from these written records. Even in the 1500s, the only people who could read and write well were usually monks, priests or nuns. Until the 1800s, there were few schools for ordinary people.

You will need: *pair of compasses, pencil, 16 x 16cm white art paper, ruler, eraser, fine-tipped artists' paintbrush, acrylic paints, gold paint, scissors, paper glue, 26 x 26cm coloured mounting card.*

1 Set your pair of compasses at a radius of 6cm. Place the point in the centre of the white art paper and draw a 12cm-diameter circle.

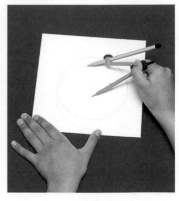

2 Keep the compasses at the same radius. Place the point 2cm away from the centre of the first circle. Draw a second circle so that it overlaps the first.

4 Rub out the circle lines to the left of the ruled lines. Use the ruler to draw two short lines to cap the top and bottom of the vertical stem of the D.

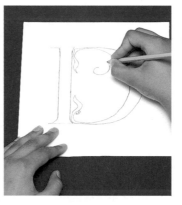

5 Extend the inner curve of the D into two squiggles at the top and bottom of the stem. Draw two simple spirals in the centre of the D.

6 Use the spirals to help you fill your design. Double the curving lines to make stems and leaves, and add petals. Look at the picture shown for ideas.

The first letter in a paragraph or on a page of an illuminated manuscript was often specially designed like this one. It was bigger and more richly decorated than other illuminated letters on the page. These letters not only made the pages look beautiful, but also made it obvious to the reader where to start reading. Decorated letters and manuscripts are called illuminated because the decorations seem to illuminate (light up) the pages. This illuminated letter comes from the Winchester Bible which was copied during the 1100s.

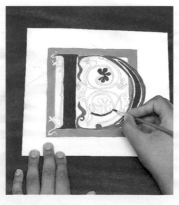

9 Paint the border first in a bright colour. Then carefully fill in the whole design. Make sure that each colour is dry before you apply the next.

10 When the paint is dry, trim the whole artwork to a 15cm square. Then colour in the gold background. Leave to dry on a flat surface.

3 Place the ruler on the left side of the circles. Draw two vertical lines from top to bottom of the circles. The lines should be about 2cm apart.

Eadwine, a monk who lived in the 1150s, is using a quill pen to write with, and holding the page steady with his knife. Quills were long bird's feathers with sharpened points. The hollow spine of the feather soaked up a little store of ink. Until about AD1000, most manuscripts were made in monasteries. The monks worked in a special room called a scriptorium. Over the decades, as the number of books increased, there was more work for professional scribes (writers). Writing gradually became a well-respected and learned profession. It developed into an art form in manuscripts illuminated with letters like the one in the project.

7 Draw two lines to the left of the vertical stem of the D. Add a squiggle and leaves top and bottom, and some decorative kinks, as shown above.

8 Use a pencil and ruler to draw a border about 1.5cm wide, as shown. Leave the right side until last. See how the curve of the D tips out of the border.

Take your time to draw and paint your illuminated letter. Monks and scribes who were experienced illustrators worked quite fast. However, they probably only managed to do two or three detailed drawings a day. There was a great deal to be done before work could start. Animal skins were scraped, soaked and dried to make parchment. This was stronger, longer lasting and more valuable than paper. A supply of feathers was dried before being sharpened into quills, and inks and colours were mixed.

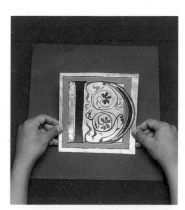

11 Paste the back surface of the artwork. Then carefully place it squarely in the centre of the richly coloured mounting card.

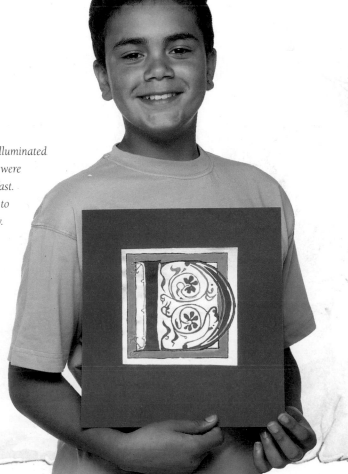

Elite Fighters

It took money, noble birth and years of training to become a knight. You also had to be male. A woman or someone from a peasant family could never be a knight. Boys from wealthy families started to train for knighthood when they were about seven years old. They were sent to another noble household to serve as pages. They also learned basic reading and writing, to sing, dance, ride a horse and fight with a sword.

At 14, a page became a squire, or apprentice, and was attached to a particular knight. He looked after his master's horses and armour and went with him into battle. Squires also learned to fight alongside other squires, pages and soldiers as part of the knight's armoured team. The training was hard and not all squires achieved knighthood. Many died in battle when they were still teenagers. After successful squires had been knighted in a formal dubbing ceremony – at the age of about 21 – they were addressed with "Sir" in front of their name.

Knights rode into battle on horseback, often in formation, in front of a back-up army of foot soldiers. They were fast, strong, skilled fighters, and well-armed compared with ordinary soldiers.

▲ A Rich Man's Work
A knight of the 1200s is in his fighting clothes, ready for battle. Medieval knights needed to be quite rich because they had to buy their own equipment. A warhorse alone cost about as much as the price of a small private plane today. Together with a full set of armour, the total cost might be about the same as a whole lifetime's wages for an ordinary farm labourer.

◀ Holy Fighters
The red cross on the knight's shield shows that he is a member of an order of monks called the Knights Templar. The name comes from the Temple of the Dome of the Rock in Jerusalem where the Order was based. The Knights promised to give up all worldly possessions and lived like monks, but they also fought in the Crusades. In the 1300s, the Pope and the king of France decided that the Knights Templar were too powerful. They accused them of not following the Christian faith, and ordered many leaders to be tortured and burned at the stake.

Gentle Pursuits ▶
A young knight shows his gentle side. Knights were expected to be bold in battle but also sporting and chivalrous. Chivalry, from the French word *cheval* (horse), originally meant horsemanship. By the 1100s it was used to describe the ideal way a knight should behave. This included being honest, courtesy to women, protecting the weak, and having respect for the church. Many knights did not meet such high standards.

LICENSED TO KILL ▶

A Japanese Samurai warrior is literally dressed to kill. A medieval Samurai was allowed to slice someone's head off just for a bit of killing practice. Later, they were only allowed to kill someone who had provoked them on a point of honour. The Samurai were warriors who served Japanese warlords, and lived with them in castles. This one is wearing the armour of a mounted warrior of the 1200s and 1300s, with shoulder and leg guards. He would have fought with bows and arrows from a distance and razor-sharp swords in close combat.

▲ ARISE SIR!

A painting of the early 1900s captures the moment when a knight is created. At a solemn dubbing ceremony, an important person, such as a monarch or a lord, rested a sword on the candidate's shoulders and declared him to be a knight. The new knight promised loyalty and to follow the code of chivalry. He was then presented with a sword and spurs. On the previous evening, he had probably taken a bath of rosewater and spent the whole night praying in the chapel, with his armour on the altar before him.

◀ EVER READY FOR BATTLE

They may be enjoying some free time away from the horrors of siege and battle, but these knights and squires are also keeping their archery skills up to scratch. Even when a castle was not at war, it had to be in a state of constant readiness in case of sudden attack. Knights and their soldiers practised fighting with staffs and swords, and moving when weighed down with heavy armour. Sports such as wrestling, throwing the javelin, stone-putting and acrobatics also kept them fit.

Festive Tournaments

Knights needed a realistic situation in which to practise their fighting skills and horsemanship. Mock battles called tournaments, tourneys or mêlées were introduced in Europe around AD1000. Two teams of mounted knights fought against each other over huge areas of countryside. The weapons they used, however, were real, and there were many injuries and deaths. The defeated knights had to give up their horses and armour to the victors. Those on the winning side could gain valuable prizes of money, warhorses and armour.

Tournaments became less bloody affairs when blunted swords and short lances were introduced in the 1200s, although there were still nasty accidents. They were like sports festivals where people went to be entertained and to be seen in all their wealth and importance. A knight could show off his skills and courage. If a lady was impressed, she might throw him a personal token of her favour, such as a piece of jewellery. Jousting, in which two mounted knights charged at each other with wooden lances and tried to unhorse each other, became a popular event. It sometimes continued as a sword fight on the ground.

▲ IDENTITY PARADE

Knights parade before the ladies at the start of a tournament held in 1390. Maybe one of the ladies will ask for her scarf to be tied to the arm of her favourite. The red barrier is called a tilt. It was set up in the jousting field – or tiltyard – to separate the opposing knights as they charged towards each other. They tilted their lances over the barrier and tried to unhorse each other.

▲ ARMOUR FOR A HORSE

A knight's horse, dressed in tournament finery, is led to the tilting field by the knight's young page. A knight's warhorse was called a destrier, and was his most important and valuable possession. The horses were large and strong but nimble, rather like the show jumping or cross-country eventing horses of today.

◀ HEAD-ON COLLISION

A knight has his last glimpse of an opponent hurtling towards him. He lowers his head to peer through the slit at the top of his helmet. The rest of his head is protected by cold, heavy steel. Moments before impact, the knight throws his head back so that his attacker's lance cannot enter the slit and pierce his eyes. With luck, it will strike his shield and splinter without dehorsing him, and he will win points.

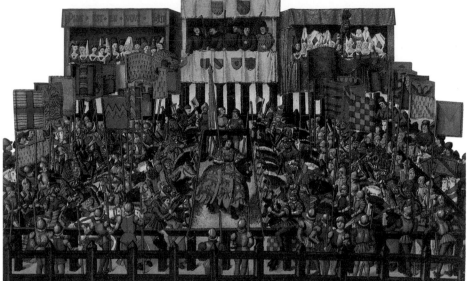

◀ LINING UP

Opposing teams face each other before a tournament battle begins. One side, armed with blunt swords and clubs, must try and knock the crests off the helmets of their opponents. The "enemy", rather wisely, have grilles fitted over their helmets to protect their faces. Attendants – who might be trainee knights such as pages or squires – stand by ready to rescue their masters if they fall. A knight of honour rides between two ropes which separate the teams.

TILTING HELMET ▶

Imagine having this heavy iron helmet on your head and trying to ride a horse at the same time! Jousting armour was heavier and stronger than battle armour to reduce the risk of injury to the competitors. Lances were often hollow so that they splintered on impact. Horses were protected with straw padding beneath their armour. If one of the knights was injured, or the jousting became a fight, judges could separate the contestants. They could also disqualify a knight for striking an unfair blow. Tournaments were supposed to be occasions of bravery and honour.

eye slit

basinet, or movable visor

▲ GOOD BEHAVIOUR

A tournament of the 1450s has been announced. Those who want to take part exchange their personal insignia (colours) with their opponents. The insignia also appeared on the knights' shields and tournament armour. They were the origin of a knight's coat of arms. The insignia were also a form of identification for the onlookers at a tournament. If a lady recognized the colours of a knight who had done something wrong, she could have him banned from the tournament.

WARMING UP ▶

Knights line up to have a go with a practice dummy, before they begin charging at each other in the real joust. If the dummy – or quintain – is not hit exactly in the centre, it swings round. If the knight does not react quickly enough, he will be knocked off his horse by the pole in the quintain's hand.

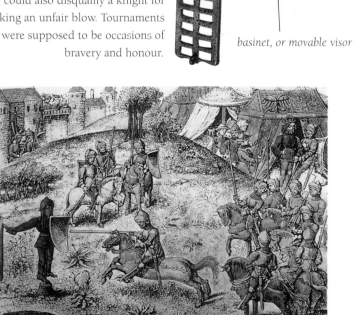

Your Personal Coat of Arms

A t the height of a battle or tourney, it was hard to recognize the different knights, especially if they were in heavy armour. Each knight, therefore, carried a shield like the one in the project, which had his own personal design on it. The same design appeared on the surcoat (overcoat) over his armour – and the surcoat became known as a coat of arms. Soon the design itself was called a coat of arms. The study of coats of arms is called heraldry, and the people who designed them were called heralds. Each design was different and recorded in books called armorials.

Draw four shield shapes on the white paper. The following steps show how coats of arms changed as the owner married, had children, and died.

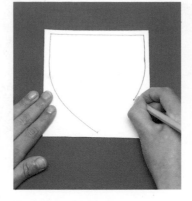

On the first shape, draw a single design on a coloured background. This is the personal symbol of a knight who has no wife or children.

You will need: *4 sheets of plain white paper approx 50 x 40cm, pencil, ruler, paintbrush, paints, two pieces of thick cardboard approx 50 x 40cm, scissors, 53 x 43cm silver paper, paper glue, five sheets of A4 paper in gold and four other different colours, masking tape.*

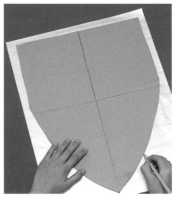

1 Draw two big shields on the thick cardboard and cut out. Mark one into quarters, and put the other to one side.

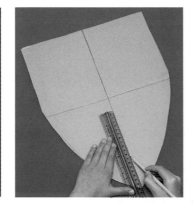

2 Place one of the shield shapes on the silver paper. Use a pencil to draw around the cardboard to make a shield outline on the silver paper.

3 Cut out the shield shape from the silver paper, 2cm from the outline. Turn the paper over and spead glue over the centre, leaving the border free.

The Sheriff of Beck's coat of arms would look impressive on a flag flying from a castle tower or as an emblem above the main entrance. The design could also be used as a personal seal to stamp on a document. At first, the monarch only granted the right to carry a coat of arms to lords and knights. Later, towns, guilds and important citizens such as the Sheriff of Beck were allowed to have them.

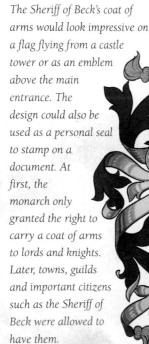

7 Draw outlines of the other quarters on the other sheets of coloured paper. Then draw in your designs for each quarter and cut them out.

8 Carefully position the designs for each quarter on to the corresponding quarter of the silver shield. Paste the designs into place.

SECOND SHIELD

For your next design, draw a line down the centre. The knight has married! Put his design on the left, and his wife's coat of arms on the right.

THIRD SHIELD

Paint a new design along the top of the next shield. Add the designs from the first two shields beneath, to show that the knight and his wife have a child.

FOURTH SHIELD

Mark the last shape into quarters. Paint the earlier designs on the left. This shows a knight's father has died. A child's personal design is on the right.

You can see how complicated the designs on a family coat of arms can become. This picture of a knight called Sir Thomas Blenerhafset is made in brass, and is placed over his grave. He wears his personal coat of arms on his surcoat and around him are the coats of arms of his ancestors. The designs have been quartered and halved again as the arms have passed from father to son. Look for the family emblems that appear in more than one design.

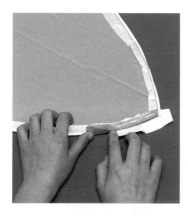

4 Lay the unquartered cardboard shield on the glued area. Make cuts along the 2cm border. Glue the edges to the back of the shield.

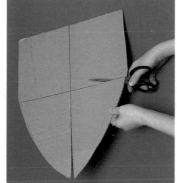

5 Take the second shield outline that you have marked into quarters. Cut out the quarters to use as templates for your design.

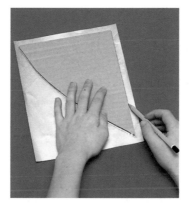

6 Place one of the bottom quarters on to the sheet of gold paper. Use a pencil to draw around the shape. Then cut out along your pencilled outline.

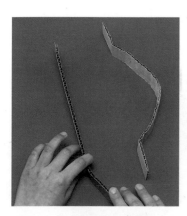

9 Cut out two 2cm-wide strips of cardboard about 30cm long. Make kinks in them about 2cm from each end to make handle shapes.

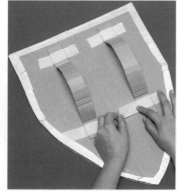

10 Turn the shield face down. Position the handles vertically in the upper part of the shield. Secure them firmly with masking tape.

Your heraldic shield may give some clues to the sort of person you are. Coats of arms often showed what a person did for a living, such as a barrel used for a wine merchant. Your coat of arms could have symbols that suggest your parents' jobs or your own interests, such as a paintbrush if you like art, or even your name. A knight's coat of arms often used traditional symbols such as lions, dragons, birds, swords, stars or flowers. The traditional colours used in heraldic designs were red, blue, black, green and purple.

Armed to the Hilt

Weapons became more deadly over the centuries and it became difficult to find armour strong enough to protect the body. Styles of armour and the materials it was made from changed to suit different ways of fighting and weapons. Chainmail was better than solid plate armour for moving around on foot or horseback. However, it did not give as much protection from arrows and spears.

The main piece of chainmail armour for early knights was a shirt called a hauberk. The metal became very hot in the sun, and so a cloth surcoat was sometimes worn. Occasionally links of the armour were driven into wounds and led to infection. Gradually, chainmail became used only for areas that needed to be flexible, like the legs and neck. In the 1300s, chest, knees, thighs and arms were protected by solid metal plates, and by the 1420s, plate armour encased the whole of a knight's body. Arrows and sword thrusts that had pierced chainmail glanced off the solid metal. To deflect gunfire, however, plate armour had to be very heavy indeed, and battles in the 1500s needed fast-moving troops. As a result, lighter armour became more common.

CHAINMAIL SKILLS ▲
A Norman soldier of the 1000s is wearing chainmail armour, split at the legs to make riding easier. Chainmail was probably made by winding wire around a rod and then cutting it into loops. Suits were shaped by increasing or reducing the number of links in a row. The Norman's shield – of wood strengthened with metal and covered with leather – was slung around his neck so that one hand was free to hold a weapon.

◀ FOLLOWING FASHION
A German soldier of the 1500s is more concerned about being fashionable than protecting himself with effective armour. Even heavy plate armour was often made to match fashionable clothes. During the Middle Ages, skilled and creative armourers were in great demand and among the most highly paid craftspeople of the time. They formed themselves into organizations called guilds. These were rather like the trade unions of today. Their aim was to encourage high standards, and to protect pay and working conditions.

HEAVY METAL ▶
A French knight and his horse of the 1290s are better protected from arrows than they would be in chainmail. The horse's legs are rather exposed to attack from foot soldiers, though. It was rare for horses to have armour, as it was very expensive. If a knight could only afford one item for his horse, he chose the chanfron (headpiece). The knight himself wore solid plate armour. This was more comfortable than chainmail, but very hot. Some knights died of heat stroke.

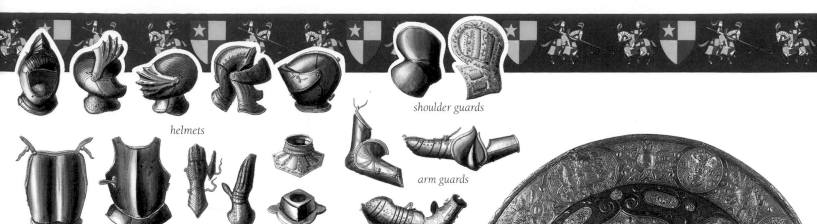

helmets

shoulder guards

arm guards

breastplates *gauntlets* *neckplates*

▲ DRESSING FOR BATTLE

Items of armour from the 1400s give an idea of how complicated it was to dress for battle. It could take up to an hour for a knight to put on his armour, because each separate piece had to be dealt with in turn. Leg armour was strapped on with leather straps or laced to the belt. Next came the breastplate and the backplate, followed by shoulder and arm pieces, and gauntlets (metal gloves). The helmet went on last.

DECORATIVE EFFECTS ▲

A splendid German shield of iron and brass has decorations that are embossed (raised from) the surface, and a roped (turned over) rim. The iron is painted, not only to make it look smart, but to preserve it. From the 1500s, when this shield was made, many new decorative techniques were being tried. The metal could be given a bluish tinge by controlled heating. Acid was used to etch (eat away) delicate designs into the surface. Edges, or sometimes whole suits of armour, were gold plated or gilded. This shield is lighter than earlier shields. In battle, soldiers had to move extremely quickly and this was not possible in very heavy armour.

▲ SPOT THE KING

King Louis XII of France sets out, dressed for battle, in 1507. The cloth over his armour was decorated with heraldic symbols, and his horse was caparisoned (wearing a heraldic covering) to match. The horse cloth is called a base. The matching outfits and the plume on the king's helmet, made it easy for soldiers to spot their leader in the height of battle.

SAMURAI ARCHER ▶

A suit of Japanese Samurai armour, of about 1652, looks very heavy to wear. It was, however, flexible enough to be worn by archers mounted on horseback. Most of the armour is made of small iron plates laced together with silk and leather and decorated with lacquer.

Head Protection

The real-life version of the helmet in this project could make the difference between life and death for a soldier in battle. However, it was made of iron and decorated with brass, and was very heavy and unwieldy. In the 1100s, a flat-topped helm (or haume) was introduced, but did not deflect sword blows and arrows as well as a rounded helmet. The 1300s brought the basinet helmet which had a moveable visor over the face. The introduction of hinges and pivots in the 1400s meant that a shaped helmet could be put on over the head and then closed to fit securely. From the 1500s, more importance was placed on a soldier's freedom of movement, so lighter, open helmets were worn. These were comfortable and soldiers could move freely around in battle.

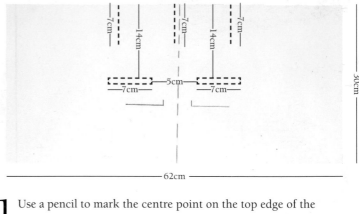

You will need: ruler, pencil, 2 sheets A1 silver card and 2 sheets A1 gold card, craft knife, cutting board, scissors, stapler, masking tape, pair of compasses, glue, brass split pins.

Can you see your helmet on a Crusader knight second from left? The illustration shows a variety of helmet, shield and spur styles between 1000 and 1400. The earliest style is on the left and the latest on the far right. Some helmets had padded linings. If not, a padded cap like the one to the left of the flag was worn. The narrow-slitted design to the right of the flag is a special helmet for jousting.

1 Use a pencil to mark the centre point on the top edge of the silver card, 31cm from the corner. With a ruler, draw a 7cm-long dotted line down from this point. Then mark two more 7cm lines 11cm to either side of the centre line, as shown. Draw eye slits, with the top edges 14cm from the top edge of the card as shown.

4 Curve the helmet to make a long tube. Staple together at top and bottom. Tape over the join with masking tape to secure and to cover the staples.

5 Set your pair of compasses at 10cm and draw a 20cm circle on the remaining silver card. Set the compasses to 9cm and draw an 18cm inner circle.

6 Cut out the big circle. Make cuts at 4cm intervals to the line of the inner circle. Bend them inwards and overlap. Tape on the inside to hold in place.

10 Cut a 62 x 2cm strip of gold card. Put spots of glue at intervals along the wrong side. Stick this gold band around the top of the helmet.

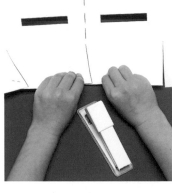

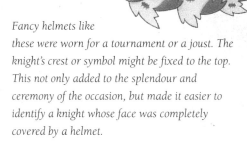

2 Use craft knife and cutting board to cut out the eye slits. Cut a 62 x 4cm strip of gold card. Align it beneath the slits. Draw the slits on the gold strip, and cut out.

3 Cut along the three 7cm lines on the silver card. Fold over the card inwards at these points to make the helmet curve. Staple the top of each overlap.

Fancy helmets like these were worn for a tournament or a joust. The knight's crest or symbol might be fixed to the top. This not only added to the splendour and ceremony of the occasion, but made it easier to identify a knight whose face was completely covered by a helmet.

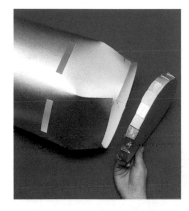

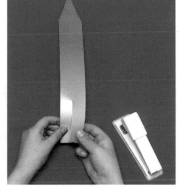

7 Put spots of glue around the outside of the helmet's rim. Hold the body of the helmet with one hand and carefully fit the top into it with the other.

8 Cut a 30 x 4cm strip of gold card with one end pointed. Cut a 7cm slit down the middle of the other end. Overlap the top of this by about 1cm and staple.

9 Staple the gold eye-slit strip into a circular band. Slip this over the helmet so the eye slits match up. Staple the nose piece in place between the eye slits.

11 Use the pointed end of compasses to make four, regularly spaced holes on each "cheek" of the helmet. Make three holes along the nose piece.

12 Push one brass split pin into each of the holes. Cover the backs with strips of masking tape so they will not scratch your face.

The Christian knights who fought in the Crusades wore helmets rather like the one you have made. In the years 1095 to 1272, lords and knights from many European countries left their castles and headed towards Palestine. Their aim was to fight Muslim armies for control of the Holy Land. The Crusader knight wore a chainmail shirt (called a hauberk) with a cloth surcoat over the top. European armourers picked up some design ideas from their Muslim enemies, who were well known for their skills in forging steel.

Weapons to Die For

Bows and arrows were the most deadly weapons of the battlefield in the days of castles. Attacks began when the armies were still distant, with a hail of arrows fired by ranks of bowmen. Skilled bowmen were well-paid and respected soldiers. As the armies drew together, the soldiers fought in close combat with hand weapons such as swords and daggers. Ordinary foot soldiers were armed with staff weapons (halberds). These were axes or hammer-like iron heads set on long poles. The blade of the halberd had the thrust of a spear and the cutting power of an axe.

Knights fought from horseback with swords and a kind of long spear called a lance. They also used battle axes, maces and flails. However, they prized their swords above all, and often had the hilt set with jewels or relics (sacred remains of a holy person). Cannons were not widely used in castle battles until the 1400s. By this time, some cannons had wheels, which made it possible to move them around.

▲ SWORDS OF HONOUR

A Samurai warrior gallops to the attack, armed with bows and arrows. As with the knights of Europe, though, the sword was the Samurai's most prized possession. The main Samurai sword was the katana. Its strong, razor-sharp blade was protected by a wooden scabbard (holder) called a saya. The hilt was covered in rough shark skin to stop the knight's hand from slipping, and bound with silk braid.

FAST-FLYING AND DEADLY ARROWS ▶

The battle is at its height. The crossbowman's weapon is powerful and extremely accurate. Now that the enemy is within 50m (the length of an Olympic swimming pool) the crossbow's deadly steel-tipped metal bolt will fly fast and pierce the strongest metal armour. Then, though, this soldier will be at risk, for it will take time and effort to reload. A windlass machine was invented that could pull back the cord quickly, making the crossbow ready to fire again.

LONGBOWS ▶

Soldiers use all their strength to draw back their bows to make the arrows fly straight and far. A good longbowman could shoot arrows about 250m (twice the length of a football pitch). This meant that soldiers could hit an attacking enemy from the safety of their castle walls. Longbows were usually made of light, pliable yew wood and were as tall as the archer himself. Up to twelve arrows could be shot from a longbow in the time it took to load and shoot one or two crossbow bolts.

◀ HAND-TO-HAND COMBAT

Imagine the dreadful cut and thrust of hand-to-hand combat from this selection of late medieval weapons. The double-edged sword, used until the late 1200s, could tear through chain mail links to drive into the body. The two-handed swords of the 1300s were better for stabbing between the gaps in plate armour. War flails were viciously whirled around. Their spiked weights caused dreadful injuries to horses and foot soldiers. Once a knight or soldier had fallen, their helmets were no protection against the blows of the mace (spiked club).

knight's sword

war flail

mace

pointed sword

▲ ARMED FOR ATTACK

The bows and arrows used by these soldiers do not look very effective against the high, strong castle walls. The archer is shooting upwards so that his arrows will fly over the walls. Small cannon were fired in this attack, at Poitiers in 1400, but they were not very accurate or powerful. The soldiers are in great danger of being hit by the castle defenders. Their only protection is the big curved shield.

◀ SOLID WEIGHT

Cannonballs of solid stone or metal, like these, could smash holes in castle walls. However, until the late 1400s, very few cannons were powerful enough to do so much damage. The first cannons used in Europe in the early 1300s were more dangerous for the people firing them. The gunpowder sometimes exploded in the barrel, killing everybody nearby. These cannonballs may have been made from lead stripped from a roof.

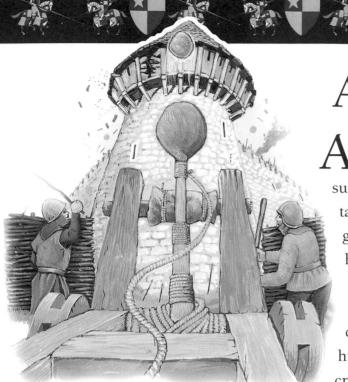

Attack and Siege

An attacking army surrounded a castle before an attack. The leader of the army might ask the people inside if they wanted to surrender without a fight. If they refused, the attackers might try to take the castle by siege. The aim was to force the inhabitants to give in by waiting for them to run out of food and water. This, however, could take a long time and be very expensive.

It was quicker for an army to take a castle by fighting its way in. Before soldiers stormed into the building, they bombarded the castle walls with weapons to weaken its defences. Boulders were hurled – from giant catapults called mangonels or trebuchets – to crash through weak spots such as the wooden roofs of towers.

Ballistas were large crossbows mounted on wheels. They fired huge, heavy bolts, often tipped with inflammable material to set the wooden parts of the castle on fire. Many siege machines were so big and heavy that they had to be made on site or dismantled and transported to the site.

If there was a moat full of water, the attackers had to fill it with stones or build a bridge – while under fire from the defenders. If there was no moat, they might tunnel beneath the castle walls to weaken them, or build a passageway into the castle. Sometimes the easiest way to enter was to bribe the guards to open the gates. During one siege, soldiers climbed up a lavatory shaft! Many castles surrendered after only a few days, or the two sides bargained with each other and made an agreement to stop fighting.

▲ FIRST SHOTS

The soldier operating this giant catapult is fairly safe at this point in the attack, as he is not too near the castle walls. The catapult can fire ammunition from quite a long distance away. His job is to help weaken the castle defences and, if possible, break through the walls to make it safer for his army to storm the castle. He might fire the head of an enemy soldier from the catapult to frighten and demoralize the castle inhabitants.

◄ TORTOISE

A moving shield creeps towards the walls of a castle. Beneath, sheltered from missiles hurled from above, is a menacing force of Roman soldiers. The giant shield resembles the shell of a tortoise and is formed from the shield of each soldier, held rim to rim, so there are no gaps for arrows or spears to fall through. The Roman "tortoise" was adopted by later armies. A variation was a wooden shelter on wheels, also called a cat, with soldiers hidden inside.

◄ VANTAGE POINT

Archers fire directly on to castle battlements from the top level of a huge tower. The belfry (siege tower on wheels) was rolled right up to the castle walls. The attackers could then lower a drawbridge from the top of the tower to the battlements and storm right into the castle itself. Each level of the tower was linked by a ladder. As soldiers on top were killed or wounded, others climbed from below to replace them. To reduce the risk of fire from flaming arrows, damp or fresh animal skins were placed on top of the wooden towers.

▲ RISKY CLIMB

French soldiers attack a position held by the English in 1443. The soldiers climbing the walls on scaling ladders are wide open to attack. The defenders on the top of the walls could easily shoot them, or throw rocks or boiling water over them. They might even push the ladders away from the walls. Sometimes large, wooden shields called mantlets were used to protect the soldiers as they scaled the walls.

◄ BATTERING RAMS

The heavy door of a castle finally gives way under the impact of a battering ram. The first rams were just heavy logs, sometimes with metal points on the end to make them stronger. It took several soldiers to lift them and swing them backwards and forwards to smash through a wall or gate. Later rams were swung from chains or mounted on wheels or rollers. Sometimes, soldiers and ram were covered by a wheeled wooden shelter called a penthouse, a tortoise, or a cat.

▲ FIGHTING MACHINE

This German fighting machine has four gun barrels as well as lethal pronged spears. By the late 1400s, gunpowder and cannons were smashing castle walls more effectively than manpowered battering rams. Gunpowder was also packed into small iron pots to make a kind of early grenade called a petard. The petard was ignited and then thrown at the enemy or placed on a bridge or gate to blow a hole in it.

Missile Attack

It took time and good planning to mount a siege attack. Giant catapults, like the one in the project, played a vital role at the beginning of a siege. Their job was to weaken the castle defences from a distance before the foot soldiers moved in close. A deadly fire of fast-flying boulders and flaming ammunition killed and maimed the fighters inside the castle walls.

The trebuchet was the most powerful of the siege machines used in the 1100s. The most powerful ones could fire rocks of up to 90kg (the weight of a large adult), over a distance greater than that covered by three football pitches.

> *You will need*: *28 x 25cm thick cardboard, ruler, pencil, craft knife, cutting board, two 28cm x 1cm lengths of balsa wood and two 16.5cm x 1cm lengths of balsa wood for base, wood glue, bradawl or pair of compasses, two 20cm x 3.5cm x 0.5cm lengths of balsa wood for side supports, 22cm x 0.5cm-diameter round balsa dowel, 32cm x 0.5cm-diameter balsa dowel, four 25cm lengths of 0.5cm² square balsa wood, string, self-hardening clay, small match box, acrylic paints, firm-bristled artist's paintbrushes.*

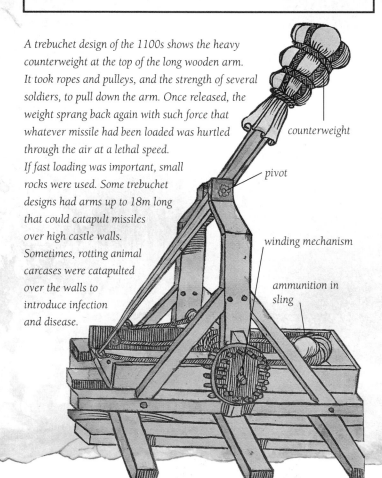

A trebuchet design of the 1100s shows the heavy counterweight at the top of the long wooden arm. It took ropes and pulleys, and the strength of several soldiers, to pull down the arm. Once released, the weight sprang back again with such force that whatever missile had been loaded was hurtled through the air at a lethal speed. If fast loading was important, small rocks were used. Some trebuchet designs had arms up to 18m long that could catapult missiles over high castle walls. Sometimes, rotting animal carcases were catapulted over the walls to introduce infection and disease.

counterweight

pivot

winding mechanism

ammunition in sling

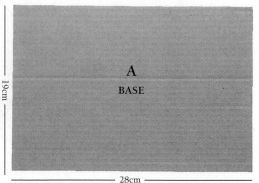
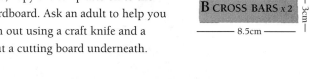

A
BASE

28cm

19cm

C CENTRE SUPPORT

16.5cm

— 3cm —

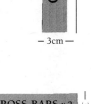

B CROSS BARS x 2

— 3cm —
—— 8.5cm ——

1 Following the measurements as shown above, copy the templates on to the thick cardboard. Ask an adult to help you cut them out using a craft knife and a ruler. Put a cutting board underneath.

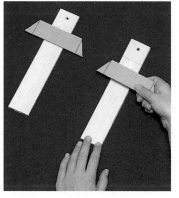

6 Lay the 20cm side supports on the work surface. Glue the crossbars into position below the holes, about 3.5cm below the top of the side supports.

7 Place four of the 25cm lengths of dowel on to the cutting board. Ask an adult to help cut both ends of the dowel pieces diagonally at a 45° angle.

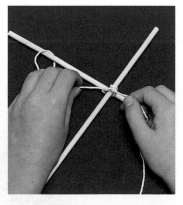

10 Make a cross with the 22cm and 32cm lengths of round dowel so that the crosspiece is about 9cm from the top. Bind together with string.

11 Put lumps of clay in the palms of your hands. Mould one big ball about 5cm in diameter, and some smaller balls, and put on one side to dry.

2 Lay the rectangular base section A on the work surface. Use wood glue to stick the 28cm and 16.5cm lengths of balsa wood along each edge of it.

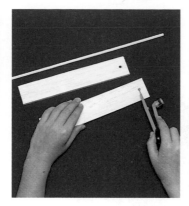

3 Use a bradawl or the sharp point of a pair of compasses to pierce a hole near the end of each of the 20cm lengths of balsa wood for side supports as shown.

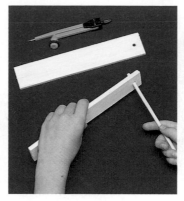

4 Wiggle the point around a bit to make the hole bigger. Push one of the pieces of balsa dowel through the holes to make them the same diameter.

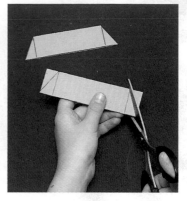

5 Use a ruler to draw a line 1cm from the end of each of the crossbar sections B. Cut diagonally from the corner to the line to make a slanting edge.

8 Glue the supports mid-way along each long side of the base. Glue the 25cm balsa strips 2.5cm from the corners, to form a triangle over the top, as shown.

9 Glue along each edge on one side of the 16.5cm centre support. Stick it into place on the side supports, about 9cm from the base.

The clay missiles fired from your trebuchet are unlikely to do much damage. However, with its long, weighted arm, and open supporting frame, the model trebuchet operates in exactly the same way as the medieval trebuchet. The word trebuchet comes from a French word for a similar device that was used for shooting birds.

12 Glue the back of the inside of the matchbox. Stick it on the end of the long arm of the cross piece. Stick the big clay ball on the other end.

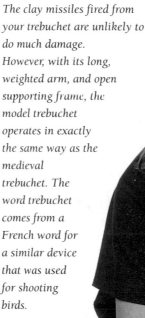

13 Fit the arms of the crosspiece into the holes in the side supports with the matchbox at the bottom. Finally, paint the model.

Defence

Inside a castle under attack, everyone fought for their lord and his lands, and for their own lives. Those in big, complex castles were in a strong position. There were plenty of ways to trap, wound or kill invaders. Defenders ran along the ramparts, dropping missiles or boiling water on to anyone attacking from below. Bowmen positioned themselves on platforms jutting out from the towers so that they could aim along the walls at those trying to scale them. The narrow slits or arrow loops in castle walls meant that bowmen could fire at the enemy, while keeping out of sight. Small gates were hard to see and easy to defend. Defenders could slip out unseen and take the groups of attackers by surprise.

The entrance of a castle was the weakest part and often the main point of attack. It was protected by a gatehouse and a heavy iron gate called a portcullis. If there was a moat, the drawbridge was raised so that the castle became an island. Inside a castle, siege towers could also be used from which to fire over the walls at the enemy. Successful defence of a castle depended on the spirit and loyalty of the soldiers, as well as a good supply of food, drinking water, weapons and missiles. The main threats were treachery, when soldiers joined the enemy, and starvation.

▲ GOING UNDERGROUND

Secret tunnels leading under the castle like this one might be made by defenders during a siege. They could smuggle in supplies of food from outside. Tunnels, however, could also be made by an attacking army. They would tunnel under the castle walls. They then set fire to the wooden poles supporting the tunnel roof and ran to safety. Both the tunnel and the castle wall above then collapsed. Many castle towers are round because they were less likely to collapse than square ones.

▲ OVERHEAD ATTACK

Boiling water and missiles were thrown through these "murder holes" in the ceiling of a castle gatehouse. Invading soldiers could be trapped in the building and attacked from above. Cold water could also be poured through these ceiling holes to put out a fire in the gatehouse.

▲ GUARDED BY WATER

The lake surrounding Bodiam Castle in England is an excellent line of defence. Castle moats made close assault with bows and arrows and siege engines difficult. It was also impossible to tunnel beneath the castle walls, as the tunnels would immediately fill with water. Attackers would have to drain, fill, or bridge a moat, or sail or swim across it under heavy fire. Many castles also had a barbican, an outer gatehouse that protected the moat and drawbridge.

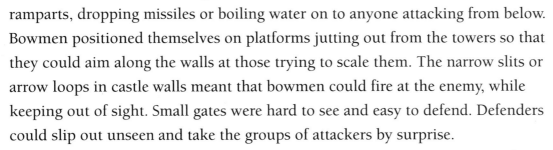

◄ HOARDINGS

Wooden hoardings jut from the towers of Liechtenstein Castle. Defending soldiers were protected in the wood-covered corridors. They could drop missiles through the holes in the floor on to the heads of attackers at the foot of the walls, without having to lean out over the battlements. They might pour hot water, red-hot sand, rocks or quicklime that burned the skin. Hoardings were often made when a battle was expected. However, they often stayed in place permanently if they were not burnt or damaged during the attack.

DOUBLE THE TROUBLE ►

The bird's eye view of Beaumaris Castle shows two lines of massive walls for double protection. If attackers breached (broke through) the outer walls, they were then trapped in the inner ring. The castle defenders could then attack them. Beaumaris Castle is on the Isle of Anglesey in North Wales. Its two sets of concentric walls were to be surrounded by a moat full of sea water. There were to be 16 towers along the outer walls and six towers on the inner circle, plus two gatehouses with double towers. However, the castle was never completed. Work began in 1295 but stopped in 1300 because the war for which it was designed had ended.

CANNONS ARE COMING ►

These cannons are on a low, round platform. This gives a wide view of the surrounding land yet makes them hard for the enemy to target. This castle was built by King Henry VIII in 1530 as part of a chain of defences along the English coast. Castles and forts had begun to be designed just for defence and lived in only by soldiers. They no longer doubled as people's homes, like typical medieval castles. Unlike siege engines, cannons could easily blast holes in walls. Traditional castles were no longer able to defend themselves effectively, and so fewer and fewer were built.

Gatehouse Defence

Castle gatehouses like the one in the project can often be seen quite clearly among the ruins of castles today. The entrance to a castle was a weak point, and needed as much protection as possible. Soldiers were permanently posted in the gatehouse. The portcullis (gate) had to be of heavy iron. The best-protected castles had a moat with a drawbridge across, that could be raised quickly in case of attack. Sometimes there was a barbican – an outer gatehouse that defended the drawbridge.

Some barbicans were connected to the castle by a narrow, roofless passage in which intruders could be attacked from above. If the situation became too dangerous for the castle inhabitants, a sally-port (a well-concealed exit), was the way to escape. Once a barbican was taken by the enemy, the attackers could get close to the main gatehouse. If that was taken the castle would be captured quickly.

> *You will need: 50 x 76cm corrugated cardboard, pencil, ruler, craft knife, cutting board, glue, large roll of masking tape, self-hardening clay, two 22cm x 0.5cm lengths of balsa wood, two 8cm lengths of 0.5cm diameter balsa dowel, kebab stick cut to 8.5cm length, 11 x 7.5cm of 0.5cm thick balsa wood, four 10cm lengths of thin chain or string, map pins, acrylic paints, one thin and one thick artist's' paintbrush.*

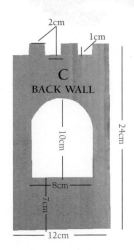

1 Following the measurements shown above, copy the templates on to the thick cardboard. Ask an adult to help you cut them out using a craft knife and a ruler. Put a cutting board underneath. If you have a big roll of masking tape, you can draw around half of the inside ring to do the arch of the gateways.

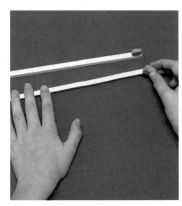

4 Soften the clay in the palms of your hands. Place on the cutting board. Use the craft knife (or ruler) to cut two 2 x 1cm box shapes about 1.5cm thick.

5 These box shapes are the counterweights for the bridge. When they are dry, glue them to the end of each of the 22cm lengths of balsa wood.

Gatehouses had to be quite large and solid buildings to house the winding mechanism of a portcullis. In this picture you can see the heavy-duty rope connected to pulleys and wound around a winch. Soldiers turned a handle to operate the winch. This pulled in the rope through the pulleys and so raised the heavy iron gate. The portcullis could be dropped shut in a hurry in case of enemy attack, with the help of heavy weights.

9 Push each end of the kebab stick into the holes in the cut edge of the corrugated cardboard. Put them at the base of the front gateway.

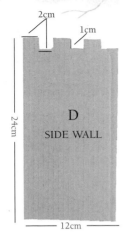

2cm
1cm

24cm
12cm

D
SIDE WALL

12cm

A
BASE X 2

12cm

2 Glue the front wall **B**, the side wall **D**, and the back wall **C** to the base **A**. When the glue is dry, put masking tape over the outside corner joins.

3 Spread glue along all but one edge of the second section **A**. Slide it horizontally into the gatehouse base, to fit just at the edge of the windows.

The portcullis slid down grooves in the gatehouse wall. The heavy iron bars were moved by ropes and winding gear. Soldiers had to close the cumbersome gate fast, to stop an enemy from entering the castle and weakening castle defences even further.

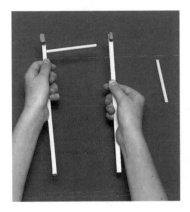

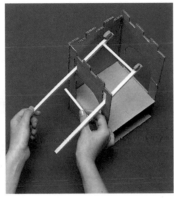

6 Glue one of the 8cm lengths of balsa on the insides of each of the 22cm lengths of dowel. Place this crosspiece 1cm below the counterweights.

7 Push the rods, from the inside of the gatehouse, through the holes on the front wall. Glue on the second 8cm dowel as shown above.

8 Glue the 8.5cm length of kebab stick to one end of the 11 x 7.5cm bridge section. It should just overlap at each side. Tape over to secure.

10 Attach one end of the chain with map pins to the ends of the kebab stick rods. Attach the other to the front corners of the bridge.

11 Cut out about ten small card rectangles about 1 x 1.5cm. Glue them in groups on the walls. Paint the gatehouse and drawbridge.

The model gatehouse is left open on one side so that you can raise and lower the drawbridge by pulling on the counter-weights. In reality, the chains would have been attached to pulleys operated from within the gatehouse or barbican.

Crime and Punishment

The owner of a castle often settled disputes among the people who lived on his lands. Only people who were believed to be a threat, such as enemy knights, were imprisoned. Other punishments were often suited to the crime committed. Someone caught stealing might have a hand cut off. A person who was causing trouble by being rude or spreading lies about someone else might lose his tongue. Serious robbery, such as stealing the castle stores or animals, or encouraging people to riot or fight against a lord, might be punished by hanging. Sometimes people paid fines of money or produce.

Few castles had specially built prisons or dungeons. Instead, store rooms or cellars that could be easily locked and secured were used. These were often below ground and were damp, dark and airless. Purpose-built dungeons were usually in or near the gatehouse where there was always a guard on duty. Those prisoners who were captured knights or noblemen were only released if their friends or relatives paid a large sum of money, called a ransom. They were treated well because they were not worth any money if they died. Sometimes they gave their word not to escape and were given the freedom to roam around the castle.

▲ **THE DOOR CLOSES**
The only way in or out is the hole in the ceiling. The prisoner is in an oubliette, named from the French word *oublier* (to forget). He is neither rich nor important. He cannot buy his way out. Friends and family might not even know where he is. Even his captors may forget he is there.

◀ **CHILLING SPOT**
Unlike many castles, sinister Chillon had a custom-built prison within its walls. This was because the castle, on the eastern shores of Lake Geneva, had been built as a fortress in the AD700s. It was later converted to a castle in the 1200s. The prison became famous when English poet Lord Byron wrote a poem called *The Prisoner of Chillon*. The poem was about a political prisoner held there in the 1500s. Chillon was protected by water on one side and by towers on the other.

◀ IN CHAINS

Very dangerous prisoners were chained up to the walls of a dungeon or prison. Their ankles might be held tightly in metal shackles, linked to a chain fixed to the wall. Sometimes, a heavy iron collar was put around their neck and again fixed to the wall with a short chain. Prisoners chained up like this could not move about.

SMALL CRIME

A person who had committed a petty crime, such as a trader selling underweight goods, was put in stocks like these. Hands or feet, and sometimes the head too, were placed in the holes, and then the top lowered and locked. People who had suffered from the prisoner's crimes – or anyone who was passing – could throw rotten food at the prisoner. A person might be locked in the stocks for a week or even longer.

▲ WARWICK CASTLE

The chill, dark dungeon at Warwick Castle, England, is below ground. It was used for keeping unimportant prisoners who were waiting for judgment of their crimes. Noble people who were being held for ransom had much more comfortable rooms, high in the tower.

CRAMPED CONDITIONS ▼

A tower near the keep of Loches Castle was a prison and torture chamber from the 1400s. One cell has a barred door of solid oak and a tiny barred window. Inside, a stone bench is the only furniture. The Duke of Milan painted pictures on the wall of his cell at Loches in the 1500s. In the Tower of London, more than 100 prisoners have scratched their names on the walls.

THUMBSCREWS ▶

Torture is a way of inflicting pain on someone to make them confess to a crime or tell secrets that they do not want to give away. Torture was unusual in castles in medieval times, but was more common in the 1600s and 1700s. One very painful method of torture used thumbscrews. These were metal rings placed around the thumbs and gradually tightened. Eventually, the thumbs were crushed if the prisoner did not start talking. Sometimes prisoners would confess to crimes they had not committed just to make the pain stop.

Timeline

The golden age of castles was between AD1000 and 1500. However, this Timeline looks back to early civilizations to find the fortresses and walled cities that preceded the medieval castle. Some of the inventions and events that affected the development of castles and the way in which they were built, are also set in the context of time and castle history.

10,000–499 BC

7000 Fortified towns with stone walls, such as Jericho, are built.

1800 Fortified city of Hattusas is built in modern-day Turkey by the kings of a warrior people called the Hittites.

1500 Great fortified palace, or citadel, of Tyrins is built by Mycenaeans on a hillside in Greece.

3000 Great walled city of Mycenae, founded in ancient Greece.

701 Assyrians use siege towers and battering rams to conquer the city of Lachish, in present-day Palestine.

the gates of Hattusas

500–1 BC

500s–400s Iron Age hill forts, such as Heuneburg hill fort in Germany, are built in Europe.

300–AD 70 Maiden Castle hill fort is built in Britain, with shelter for about 5,000 people.

214 Emperor Shih Huang-di orders the building of the Great Wall of China, stretching for 63,300km, to defend China from nomad invasion. Millions of people build the wall by hand.

35 King Herod of Judea builds the fortress palace of Masada in the mountains south of Jerusalem.

iron age hill fort

911–999

911 A band of Northmen (Vikings) is given part of France, which is then called Northmannia (present-day Normandy), to rule and settle. Early castles in Normandy are simple enclosures with gatehouses, some stone and some timber.

950 Earliest known simple stone tower is built on the banks of the River Loire at Doue-la-Fontaine, France.

950–1020 Nobles fortify their houses, with or without royal permission, building castles such as Loches in France.

998 Byzantine engineers fortify Antioch on a scale that amazes the Crusaders 100 years later.

Viking fort

1000–1079

1000s Japanese warrior lords, called Samurai, begin to control whole provinces of the country.

1000s Tournaments begin for knights to practise their battle skills and for entertainment.

1000s The Normans start to build castles in many parts of Europe, including motte and bailey castles.

1050 Norman lords build defensive castles such as Ludlow along the border between England and Wales.

1066 William the Conquerer invades England and starts building castles to defend the lands he wins.

1070 Square keep castles are built, including the White Tower in London.

Samurai warrior

motte and bailey castle

1080–1100

1086 The Domesday Book is compiled, providing a record of land use, ownership and population at a time when many castles were being built.

1099 First Crusaders capture Jerusalem from the Muslims. Europeans take eatern ideas and technology on building and defence back to their homelands.

1100 German lords begin to build tall, slender towers (*Bergfrieder*), often sited on high, craggy hills for natural defence.

1100 Shell keeps and mottes (earth mounds) surrounded by a circular stone wall – start to be built. Stone curtain walls begin to replace the earlier wooden palisade fences.

1100s Siege catapult called a trebuchet is first used.

trebuchet

1190–1200

1190 The Teutonic Order of Knights is founded in Germany. They build castles to defend the route across Europe to Christian lands in Syria and Palestine.

1190s Courtyard castles are built as the focus of defence shifts away from the great tower.

1200s Plate armour is added to chainmail. Short lances and blunted swords are now used for tournaments.

1200s Rounded wall towers are built, and brick castles appear in the Netherlands.

Harlech castle

1201–1212

1204 Fourth Crusade called by Pope Innocent III: Constantinople is captured by the Crusaders.

1206 Mongols under Genghis Khan begin conquest of Asia.

1211 Children's Crusade sets out from northern and western Europe to win back Jerusalem from the Muslims.

1213–1254

1215 Signing of the Magna Carta in which the English King John promises to give more power to English barons.

1207–1272 Reign of Henry III of England, who adds the second of three concentric curtain walls around the White Tower of the Tower of London.

1220–1250 Reign of Frederik II, the Holy Roman Emperor, who builds numerous castles in Germany and Italy.

1229 Sixth Crusade, in which Emperor Frederik II, cunningly regains Jerusalem and is crowned king.

1248–1254 Seventh Crusade to Egypt, led by King Louis IX of France.

brave knight

1341–1400

1346 At the Battle of Crecy, English archers defeat French knights, marking the gradual waning of the knight's power in battle.

c.1350 The first firearms – cannons loaded by pushing gunpowder down the barrel with muzzles – are used in Europe.

1347–1351 The Black Death kills 25 million people across Europe.

1367 Civil war breaks out in Spain, with France and Britain backing different sides.

1385 Bodiam castle is built in England because of fears of a French invasion – which never happens.

tournament battle

1401–1453

1415 At the Battle of Agincourt, English archers and horse soldiers defeat the heavily armoured French. Mounted knights are used less and less as a fighting force.

1418 Chateau Gaillard France, is besieged by the English for 16 months. The castle finally surrenders because of lack of water.

mid-1400s Fortified manor houses are built in brick at Hestmonceaux, Caister and Tattershall in England and in Holland.

1453 Ottoman Turks capture Constantinople marks the end of the Byzantine Empire and the Middle Ages.

1453 End of Hundred Years War between England and France.

1454–1510

1464 The capture of a Scottish border castle using just two cannons, marks the decline of castles as defensive homes.

1475 El Real de Manzanares is built north of Madrid.

1476–1477 Pikemen and gunners have greater effect than knights, in battles between Austria and France over Burgundy.

c.1490 Inca Fortress of Sacsayhuaman at Cuzco, Peru, completed, with 18m-high walls with giant blocks of stone weighing up to 200 tonnes each.

1509–1547 Henry VIII of England builds coastal artillary forts such as Deal, with garrisons of soldiers.

Sacsayhuaman castle

AD 0–349

43 THE ROMAN CONQUEST OF BRITAIN begins. Rome eventually controls the whole island south of Scotland.

117 ROMAN EMPIRE reaches its greatest size under Emperor Trajan, stretching for 4,000km from east to west.

122 ROMAN EMPEROR HADRIAN orders building of Hadrian's Wall, stretching for 120km across Northern Britain. The wall is to keep out the barbarian tribes, such as the Picts.

324 THE EMPEROR CONSTANTINE moves the capital of the Roman Empire from Rome to the ancient Greek city of Byzantium. This marks the founding of the Byzantine Empire, which lasted until 1453. Constantine renames the city, Constantinople in 330 and dies in 1395.

Roman fort

350–599

350 SIEGE CATAPULTS are invented.

400s BRITISH COMMANDER, ARTORIUS (ARTHUR), wins great battles against the invading Jutes, Angles and Saxons in southern Britain.

412 EMPEROR THEODOSIUS constructs protective walls around Constantinople.

442 ROMAN TROOPS leave Britain.

476 END OF THE ROMAN EMPIRE in western Europe.

500s STIRRUPS ARE INVENTED in China (introduced to Europe 700). Warriors can now fight on horseback more securely.

600–910

674–678 ARABS BESIEGE Constantinople by land and sea but fail to take the city.

800s FEUDALISM DEVELOPS IN EUROPE. Land-owning monarchs and nobles rent out strips of land to peasants and give privileges to the first knights in return for loyalty in battle.

feudalism

800–1150 ROMANESQUE STYLE OF architecture (based on the Roman style) is fashionable in Europe. In castles, this style includes round-headed arches and windows, and barrel vaults.

900 MAORIS OF NEW ZEALAND build hill-top fort villages, called *pas*, but there are no battlements for protection.

1101–1130

1113 THE KNIGHTS OF ST JOHN, or Knights Hospitaller, are founded in Jerusalem and build some of the biggest castles in the area.

1118 FOUNDATION OF THE KNIGHTS TEMPLAR, an order of fighting monks who protect the Christian pilgrims in the Holy Land.

1127 SQUARE KEEP AT ROCHESTER is built. It signalled a new era for the keep (stone donjon) as the strong point of the castle.

1130 POPE INNOCENT II bans tournaments because he thinks knights should not die fighting for sport and entertainment.

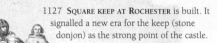
Knights of St John

1131–1149

1140s EUROPEAN CRUSADERS build several castles in the eastern Mediterranean to guard the route to the Holy Land. The most common design is a rectangle with a tower at each corner.

1142 KRAK DE CHEVALIERS, in Syria, is taken over by Crusaders. They rebuild it into a formidable castle that would withstand many attacks and sieges and greatly influence European castle building.

1142 KERAK CASTLE is built. It lasts until 1188, when it falls after an eight-month siege by the Muslim leader, Saladin.

1147–1148 SECOND CRUSADE is organised by St Bernard of Clairvaux.

Krak de Chevaliers Castle

1150–1189

1150–1500 GOTHIC STYLE OF ARCHITECTURE becomes fashionable in Europe. Features are pointed arches and ribbed vaults.

1150–1250 HOLY ROMAN EMPERORS build castles all over Germany. Frederick II of Hohenstaufen also builds castles in Italy.

1180s CASTLES WITH SQUARE WALL towers are built.

1187 MUSLIM RULER SALADIN defeats the Crusader States and re-takes Jerusalem.

1189–1192 THIRD CRUSADE fails to re-capture Jerusalem. Richard I of England reaches a truce with Muslim leader, Saladin.

Gothic style of architecture

1255–1280

1261 THE CHRISTIANS finally lose Jerusalem to the Muslims.

1267 EDWARD I OF ENGLAND passes laws to control tournaments because the events always cause terrible riots.

1268–1271 CAERPHILLY CASTLE in South Wales is built by Gilbert de Clare during his struggles with the Welsh prince Llywelyn ap Gruffydd.

1270 CAERPHILLY CASTLE, which is the largest, strongest castle built in Wales, is destroyed by Prince Llywelln ap Gruffydd.

1271 KRAK DE CHEVALIERS falls to the Muslims.

1279-1368 MONGOLS UNDER KUBLAI KHAN overthrow China, but fail to conquer Japan.

1280s EDWARD I OF ENGLAND starts building concentric castles in England and Wales.

El Real de Manzanares Castle

1281–1300

1283 CAERNARFON CASTLE begins in North Wales, together with a walled town.

1285 MUSLIMS CAPTURE MARQAB (or Margat) castle by mining beneath it.

1291 SURRENDER OF ACRE to Sultan al-Ashraf, marks the end of the Crusades.

tournament horse

1295–1330 BEAUMARIS CASTLE (a concentric castle) is built in Wales.

1300s RULES FOR TOURNAMENTS are implemented to decide the winner in friendly combat.

1300–1350 TOWER HOUSE CASTLES play an important role in the Scottish Wars of Independence.

1301–1340

1304 MORE SOPHISTICATED siege machines, such as catapults, become widespread.

cannon

1320s CANNONS FIRST USED in Europe.

1327 PFALZGRAFENSTEIN CASTLE built on an island in the middle of the River Rhine by King Ludwig I of Bavaria.

1330 PLATE ARMOUR gradually becomes widely used.

1337–1453 THE HUNDRED YEARS WAR between France and England stimulates castle building and developments.

plate armour

1511–1600

1518–1527 CHATEAU D'AZAY-LE-RIDEAU is built in France, with large windows, comfortable state rooms and defensive-style features that are purely decorative..

1576 ODA NOBUNGA, a Japanese warlord, builds a castle palace at Azuchi with a seven-storey tower, moats and stone walls.

1576-1578 CASTLE FORTRESSES Azuchi and Osaka, are built in 1576 and 1578 in Japan.

1600s GREAT AGE OF CASTLE BUILDING in Japan. European castles in Scotland, France and Germany survive as the picturesque residences of wealthy aristocrats.

1600s

1603 NIJO CASTLE is built in Japan using a framework of strong wooden beams.

1607 JAMES FORT IS established on the banks of a river in Virginia, North America, with a stockade enclosing a cannon, church, well, and small houses.

1615 TOKUGAWA IEYASU forbids castle building in Japan because "high walls and deep ditches are the cause of great upheavals when they belong to others."

1621 LAST OF THE OLD-STYLE TOURNAMENTS is held in England.

Himeji Castle

1700s TO 1900s

1798 KNIGHTS HOSPITALLER surrender Malta to Napoleon Bonaparte.

1800s RENEWED INTEREST IN CASTLES as symbols of the medieval world.

1869–1892 NEUSCHWANSTEIN Castle is built in Germany by King Ludwig II.

1971 WALT DISNEY builds a magical castle as part of a children's theme park.

Cinderella's Palace

GLOSSARY

arrow loop
A narrow slit in castle walls through which arrows were fired.

ashlar
Squared blocks of smooth stone, also called dressed stone.

bailey
An open area enclosed by the castle walls.

ballista
A large crossbow on wheels.

barbican
A wall or tower which protected a castle gatehouse from attack.

baron
A powerful man given large amounts of land by the king in return for support and soldiers.

barracks
A building where soldiers live.

battering ram
A huge tree trunk or wooden beam with a metal tip used for knocking down castle gates or walls.

battlements
The top part of a tower or wall with a series of gaps for defenders to shoot through.

belfry
A tall, wooden siege tower on wheels, often with a drawbridge on top and a covering of animal hides.

Byzantine Empire
The eastern half of the Roman Empire, which lasted for more than 1,000 years, from about AD395 to AD1453.

chainmail (or mail) Armour made of linked rings, or chains, of metal.

chaplet
A wide, ornamented padded roll worn on the head.

chivalry
Rules of polite and honourable behaviour that knights were supposed to follow.

Christian
A follower of the teachings of Jesus Christ.

citadel
A fortified stronghold, often a palace, within or close to a city.

coat of arms
The badge or special pattern of a nobleman or his family.

concentric castle
A castle with two or more rings of defensive stone walls.

corbel
A stone or wooden bracket sticking out from a wall to support a beam or other weight.

courtyard castle
A castle with a courtyard surrounded by a stone wall.

crenel
A gap in the battlements.

Crusades
Religious wars between Christians and Muslims for control of the Holy Land (today covering parts of Israel, Jordan and Syria).

drawbridge
A bridge across a moat or pit that can be lifted to make crossing impossible.

dubbing
A ceremony in which a king, queen, lord or lady gives another person the title of knight, usually by tapping them on the shoulder with a sword.

dungeon
The modern word for the area of the castle used to keep prisoners.

feudal system
The social system in the Middle Ages, through which people were granted land and protection in exchange for providing services, such as growing food or fighting.

fort
A military base for soldiers and supplies.

garderobe
A castle toilet.

garrison
The soldiers in a castle.

gatehouse
A building at the entrance to a castle, usually heavily fortified.

halberd
A sharp blade attached to a wooden pole.

hauberk
A coat or shirt of chainmail.

hennin
A tall, cone-shaped headdress made of cloth.

heraldry
The rules controlling the use of, or the study of, coats of arms on flags, armour and shields.

hoarding
A wooden extension built out from the top of a castle wall, used for firing or dropping missiles.

joust
A contest, put on for entertainment, in which one knight tries to knock the other off his horse.

keep
The strong inner, or great, tower of a castle.

knight
An important medieval soldier who fought on horseback. He received land if he promised to fight for a lord.

lance
A spear used as a weapon in war, or long, pointed pole used by knights in jousts.

lord
Any powerful male noble, knight or king, often the owner of a castle.

machicolations
The openings in the floor of an overhanging stone structure, used for dropping missiles on the enemy.

mangonel
A giant catapult, which used the power in a twisted cord to throw stones at castle walls.

manuscript
Book written by hand. From the Latin *manus* (hand) and *scriptus* (written).

mason
A skilled person who works to shape stone.

medieval
From the Middle Ages.

merlon
The raised wall between two crenels along a castle's battlements.

Middle Ages
The period from about AD1000 to 1500.

moat
A ditch full of water around a castle.

Moors
The Muslim ruling class of Spain during the Middle Ages, who came from North Africa.

mortar
A mixture of lime, sand and water that holds stone together.

motte
A tall mound of earth on which some early castles were built.

murder hole
An opening in the roof above the main gate of a castle through which defenders could fire or drop missiles on to the enemy.

Muslim
A member of the Islamic religion, started by Muhammad in AD622.

oilette
A round opening at the base of a loophole, or narrow slit in a castle wall.

oubliette
A tiny prison cell where prisoners could be forgotten about. From the French word *oublier* (to forget).

page
A young boy of noble birth who served in the household of a lord and sometimes became a squire.

peasant
A poor country person who lived by farming.

plate armour
Fitted body armour made from steel sections.

portcullis
A wooden and metal grille which was lowered down to block a castle gateway.

putlog holes
Holes in castle walls used to support scaffolding.

quicklime
A dangerous white powder that burned skin and clothing.

quintain
A target used for jousting practice.

Samurai
A Japanese mounted warrior, similar to a European knight.

siege
The surounding of a castle to cut off its supplies and make the people inside surrender, with or without a fight.

squire
A knight's servant who hoped and trained to become a knight himself.

surcoat
A loose tunic without sleeves, worn over armour.

tapestry
A decorative wall hanging, woven from coloured thread.

tournament
An event where knights jousted and fought for entertainment and to practise for real battles and wars.

tourney
A mock battle in a tournament.

trebuchet
A large catapult used for throwing rocks and other missiles at the enemy.

trencher
A slice of stale bread used as a plate.

troubadour
A travelling poet-musician of the middle Ages.

windlass
A winding mechanism, such as that which was used to tighten crossbow strings.

INDEX